The
ART
of
Automation

Leverage for companies, managers and testers

PETER MUSZKA

Contents

Legal Disclaimers

permit persons to whom the Software is furnished to do so, subject to the following conditions:

The above copyright notice and this permission notice shall be included in all copies or substantial portions of the Software.

THE SOFTWARE IS PROVIDED "AS IS", WITHOUT WARRANTY OF ANY KIND, EXPRESS OR IMPLIED, INCLUDING BUT NOT LIMITED TO THE WARRANTIES OF MERCHANTABILITY, FITNESS FOR A PARTICULAR PURPOSE AND NONINFRINGEMENT. IN NO EVENT SHALL THE AUTHORS OR COPYRIGHT HOLDERS BE LIABLE FOR ANY CLAIM, DAMAGES OR OTHER LIABILITY, WHETHER IN AN ACTION OF CONTRACT, TORT OR OTHERWISE, ARISING FROM, OUT OF OR IN CONNECTION WITH THE SOFTWARE OR THE USE OR OTHER DEALINGS IN THE SOFTWARE.

Dedication

For everyone who ever wished their hard work to be

easier

Foreword

This book is aimed to be a Quick Start Guide to Automation for companies, managers, and testers. It's intentionally short and to the point.

Different depths and levels of automation results in my concept of 5 Levels of Automation, which I will introduce you, and take you through each level chapter by chapter. I will try my best to describe these significant topics in a non-technical way, but at the same time, I will touch many technical points for engineers who would want to try out some of the ideas mentioned in this book.

The first half is theoretical with conventional tools and techniques, the second half are examples and implementation hints. I made this book purposefully light at the start, and gradually diving into more complex topics, so I would be glad if you read it through as it is.

But if you sense a burning curiosity, feel free to jump through sections.

Introduction

We could compare automation to a built up leverage. That's what people do when they automate executable steps or process. They are progressively building up leverage for themselves, for the company, team, product owner, business owner, and for customers. There is a huge pressure in IT to deliver fast, be cheap, and at the same time maintain top quality.

That will, of course, exclude one of these three needs, but it's still required. You see, these are three areas where with two assumptions you exclude the third. If it's good, then it cannot be cheap (or could, but will take longer to deliver). If it's good and fast at the same time, it must be more expensive.

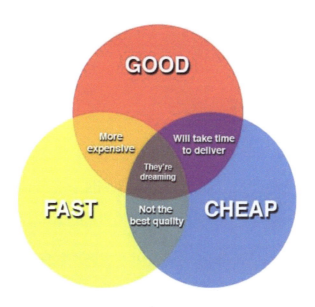

Image concept with permission from Jennifer Kes Remington

In this book, I'm writing about adding huge value. Combining Quality Assurance (QA) with Full Automation Testing (FAT). So, accordingly to this intersection, it must be more expensive. After reading this book through and implementing the core ideas, you can be confident going to your boss and describe how much Good and Fast values you are creating and adding to the company, and if he or she doesn't give you a substantial raise, you can easily switch wherever they value your work, skills, and qualities more. Or start a business on your own, where you apply your acquired skills.

Core values of this book and the ideas behind it should move you to achieve your higher goals. It's not just about programming, scripting and how to build full automation test coverage from scratch. It's also about problem-solving, being more adaptive, resourceful, team spirit, dedicated, and patient.

Essentially, it should teach you to get out of your comfort zone and try things out. Search for it, ask your team members, make research, watch a couple of video courses, fail fast and adapt. You can eventually move on to achieve your dreams in your spare time, building up your own software and applications, or websites with complex implementation.

Really the sky is the limit. Being FAT - a Full Automation Tester means, that as time goes on you really learn a lot.

You learn a lot about back-end, databases, API services, front-end, security, mobile devices, performance, integration, and understanding, and testing applications end-to-end. At the same time, you will learn to effectively communicate with your team members and customers, your nerves will be stronger, and you will acquire a bunch of valuable qualities, just as your automation tests.

We will also touch how our knowledge fits the upcoming era of Robotic Process Automation (RPA), Automated Machine Learning to Artificial General Intelligence.

Welcome to the next episode of humans collaborating with machines, bringing out the best qualities from both worlds to the surface. Keep Calm, and Keep Coding.

Giving honor to the companies where I could acquire all the necessary knowledge – Global Logic, Ness KDC, Solar Turbines, and Solar Digital, I start the name of my book with the word ART.

Our huge planning events taking place in San Diego and Kosice every 4 months has a similar name – ART PIPE, meaning Agile Release Train Product Increment Planning Event. At the time I'm writing this book we already had an amazing ART PIPE 6 in San Diego.

It has another profound meaning to it as well, as you will find out reading through the chapters until the very end.

Why automation

Well, you have certainly heard, experienced or saw it in documentary films that we live in an era of Automation, Autonomous Cars and Devices, Robotics, Machine Learning, and Artificial Intelligence. They try to scare people that Intelligent Software or Machines will eventually replace human resources. This is a real threat and could be closer than we think.

But this book is not aimed to frighten you. More than anything it has an ambitious goal to prepare and encourage you, motivate and give you a heads-up about some crucial questions that we will all soon face.

Here is a short list of jobs, in which already thousands of people got replaced by robots and software just in recent years. Some might be soon replaced on a bigger scale:

Inventory Management, Warehouse Organizing

Quality Control, Packaging, Packing, Cashiers

Phone operators, Automated Calls

Information Gathering and Analysis

Assisted writing, Content Creating

Copywriting, Stock Trading

Medical Treatments, Prescription

Taxi drivers, Truck drivers

Pilots, Bartenders, Waitresses

The question is, *"Why automation?"*

First, I want you to get rid of all preconceived fears that machines and software will eventually replace most people, and our own expertise will be unnecessary. It's not that simple, and certainly, humans *collaborating* with machines and software have more positives, then machine or software working *just by themselves*. We will dive more to this critical point throughout the book multiple times.

Manual, repetitive, hard jobs are usually cheap, but require a lot of workers who compete on the market. They can be easily replaced.

Companies compete in the same way. To survive they want to *increase efficiency, increase speed* and *decrease cost*, so they are looking for ways *to automate* and leverage these hard, repetitive jobs with software and machinery. Those are usually more efficient, faster and cheaper.

Software and machines don't need a day off when they are tired, don't need a lunch break and can work and be focused day and night 24/7. They certainly don't have personal or family problems. Once it's built and put to place, it's usually doing the same job more effectively, and the business owner will get his return on investment fast.

The key missing part here is *collaboration*, for which we will keep coming back. *Human* and *Software* collaborations have such valuable benefits, that I will cheer and emphasize around it throughout the whole book. Perhaps you will soon see and cherish it as well.

If you are automating or you are just starting, huge congratulations for you. You are creating valuable leverage, you are *saving time* and *energy* for yourself, your colleagues, and for the company. Most likely you will hugely contribute to fast product delivery on the market. Or enhance corporate process flows, so corporate life will seem super smooth.

If you don't automate, but you are curious, I want to encourage you. Robotic Process Automation is already the next big thing, and every department in corporations will implement it on some scale. It will save many people from repetitive, perhaps boring jobs, and at the same time it will create new opportunities and will require collaboration with software.

Good thing is, skillful people are the ones who are required to automate and create smart software and machinery. And *Human - Software* collaboration is crucial to maintain, enhance, oversee and control these automated leverages. Basically to bring up *new values* to the surface.

Corporate hierarchy

If you look at big organizations, they have many departments and divisions. IT is similar, with a board of directors, president, vice-president, managing director, senior program directors, project managers. Below this top level are many teams which include planners called Scrum Masters, and in each team - Tech Lead, Developers divided into front-end and back-end, Quality Assurance divided to Automation and Manual Testers.

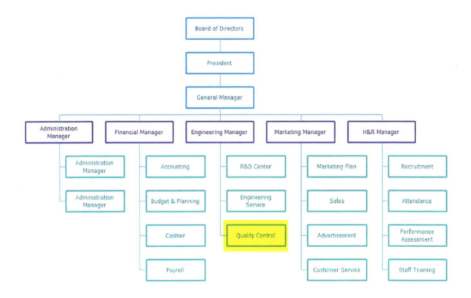

Image concept from Bryan Lamb's Udemy course:

Robotic Process Automation – RPA Overview

We will take a deeper look at organization departments and where automation has an impact from two perspectives:

Automation Testing *in an engineering software team*
Robotic Process Automation *in a specific department*

The main difference between the two is in a set of tools, frameworks or technologies in which you build your automation steps. But eventually, you can combine. Other difference is how much you need to maintain, extend, fix steps and code.

Automation Testing in an engineering software team

Is about new products going to market. In IT these are Web applications, desktop or mobile applications, APIs. It will change and adapt as time goes by and could have more features (versions) in the near future. You will need to change, adapt, extend, maintain, evaluate your tests and create reports on a regular basis. It's a part of Quality Control (QC) or Quality Assurance (QA).

Automating tests for QA means progressively building up test coverage for every application part under test. Such as API, UI, Mobile, Integration, Performance, Security, Stability.

Robotic Process Automation in a specific department

Is about faster and more precise execution of daily tasks. It's about automated software for searching and filling out tables, contacting persons or copying and verification of data from one system to another. It can have an impact on accounting, payroll, attendance, customer service, marketing plan, budget calculation, etc. It could eventually fully adopt in banking, insurance, manufacturing, healthcare, legal issues.

More advanced RPA can include machine learning capabilities and specialized artificial intelligence to some degree. It could be a part of any division in a corporate, such as Administration, Finance, Engineering, Marketing, H&R. Further divisions of these perspectives below.

Full Automation Testing includes:

Back-End – Database

Web services – API

Front-End – UI

Mobile devices

Security

Integration

Performance

Robotic Process Automation targets:

Database Access and **Read**

API - Create, **R**ead, **U**pdate, **D**elete

Data Management in readable formats

Speech – Image – Facial recognition

OCR – Optical **C**haracter **R**ecognition

MS Office, **PDF** read and write

Web, Email analysis and response

Quality Control, Quality Assurance, Testing

When you look at IT corporate hierarchy, Quality Control or Quality Assurance is on the lowest level in engineering software teams or companies in general. That was one of the things which bothered me looking at hierarchy charts, especially when they stuck a huge poster of all teams in each office, and you are at the bottom. That's a reminder that you are still a small fish in a big ocean, but that's okay.

It was a hint for me, that despite I'm doing all this up-to-date fancy Full Automation Testing, I'm still counted low, if not lowest. It might also look, that compared to the huge required skill set and qualities needed it's not paying enough. It might be the case with manual testing, but not with automation. You can make more money than most Junior developers with 1-3 years of experience if you are good. But you will need to speak up about the values you are creating if you actually creating them. Otherwise, they would just overwhelm you with work for a low paycheck.

Despite all that, I want to encourage you that there are many places you can jump to from this position. Automating any part of applications means that you must learn how the domain works. Especially for responsive web applications which have several integrated capabilities. You will need to acquire software knowledge in-and-out.

With API testing and HTTP protocol you will learn how cookies, request methods – POST, GET, PUT, DELETE – and responses work with many status codes meanings. This is called Web service or API Testing. You might need to look in the database from time to time, so you learn about Tables and Selects. And UI is all about elements, and troubleshooting requests and responses working in the background.

So, don't be sad about corporate hierarchy - your valuable skill set, technical insight and personal qualities which you acquire will worth a hundred times more than any position on a fancy chart. Because then you will have many options, and many values to give, and ideas to follow.

Levels of Automation

I briefly mentioned all 5 Levels of Automation in the Introduction section. In this chapter, we will have a deeper look.

This concept of 5 Levels of Automation in a triangle means, that each layer builds on top of all previous layers. So, if you want to become a master of Level 2 FAT – Full Automation Testing, first you need to start with Level 1 QA - Quality Assurance and become a master of that subject.

ARTIFICIAL
INTELLIGENCE
KINGDOM

MACHINE
LEARNING MASTERY

ROBOTIC PROCESS
AUTOMATION

FULL AUTOMATION TESTING

QUALITY ASSURANCE

It also nicely describes, that there are a lot of Quality Assurance experts on the market, focusing on manual or semi-automation testing, a much less Full Automation Testing experts, and so on with less Robotic Process Automation experts, Machine Learning Masters, and just a few Artificial Intelligence Crowned Kings.

Level 1 Quality Assurance - QA

This level includes a combination of Manual Testing and Semi-Automation, handling requests and responses, uploading – changing – exporting data, with manual evaluation. QA Engineers are creating scenarios with Test Steps and for some steps implementing code which will run automatically when started. In IT typical tools used are from SmartBear or one of its parts as RadyAPI and SoapUI. SahiPro is similar, and JMeter for performance measurements.

Level 2 Full Automation Testing - FAT

This level includes automation scripts and programming code for each test step, to verify and test the whole application. Database tables and selects, API raw data, UI functionality, Responsive Web apps on Mobile and Tablet, Native apps on Mobile and Tablet, Security access levels, Integration with other platforms, Performance measurements for requests and responses, Load and Penetration tests. In IT typical languages used are Java, Python, Robot, C#, Ruby and typical frameworks are TestNG, JUnit, Cucumber, Gauge, Selenium WebDriver, Appium, Sikuli Image Recognition. The whole process of deployment and testing is usually also automated with Jenkins, Puppet or Azure.

Level 3 Robotic Process Automation - RPA

RPA includes automated bots, which are performing daily basis tasks in any corporate division. They are systems based on rules - receiving emails with an invoice, extracting data, typing that into bookkeeping system or database, automated bots to respond, filling out Excel spreadsheets, copying data from one system to another. It can be described as a repeating set of actions based on rules, so we are still in a zone of "Rule-Based Automation".

To be a master of Level 3 RPA – Robotic Process Automation, several years of experience with QA and FAT might be necessary. Nowadays the IT market recognizes a new generation of RPA 2.0 as Unassisted RPA, which might require FAT skills and Business Process Knowledge in more depth. In IT typical tools used are Automation Anywhere, Blue Prism, Foxtrot, UiPath with a combination of any Full Automation Testing programming language and framework mentioned above.

Level 4 Machine Learning Mastery – MLM

Includes training specialized mathematical models which can evaluate newly uploaded data with a probability, and decides if that data (pictures, sound, videos, documents) falls to one of several categories. Mastering this level means, that we are no longer in "Rule-based" zone, but in "Learning and Differentiation" zone. These programs are also automated and learned in such scale, that can end-to-end apply machine learning, with faster creation and simpler solutions – this is called Automated Machine Learning, or AutoML.

For example, take Steganography – hiding secret messages in data (for example pictures) and Steganalysis – attacking communication channels, catching that data (pictures), and being able to tell with a probability if that picture has or has not a secret message inside it. More sophisticated Machine Learning Mastery with AutoML could search data, create data sets, create ML algorithms, and after decision making try to extract, reconstruct, read, and evaluate secret messages.

In IT typical languages used are Python, R, Scala and typical tools and frameworks are MatLab, TensorFlow. For Python popular tool is Jupyter notebook, including Anaconda and libraries NumPy, SciPy, RLPy, Keras, SciKit-Learn. There is also Eclipse Deeplearning4j, for JVM Eclipse RL4J, for AutoML Eclipse Arbiter, and many more. No worries, we will get to that. Machine Learning is really complex.

Level 5 Artificial Intelligence Kingdom - AIK

Aims for making computers think in a similar manner as a person would think. A bit scary, since such AI can have strong male precedence regarding human resources (as Amazon learned in 2015) or have sexist and Neo-Nazi views on social media (as Microsoft learned with their chat robot in 2016).

On a positive side, we have already witnessed several powerful Artificial Narrow Intelligence, like Deep Blue from IBM in 1997, AlphaGo from Google DeepMind In 2016. And I'm sure we can expect in near future perfected versions of Amazon's Alexa and Apple's Siri, enhanced self-driving cars and many more. Chinese electric car company NIO has its own Artificial Intelligence Assistant called Nomi.

We not really talk about a super intelligent all-knowing software which takes over the world (bad-tempered AGI - Artificial General Intelligence), as described in sci-fi movies and books. More likely sophisticated automated software for a small niche market. What is crucial is, that it's able to change and adapt on its own, but our own personal behavior, prejudice, and views will have a great impact on it.

By itself, it constantly runs and creates automated Machine Learning models to differentiate between many ideas. It works with probabilities or rewards, and nothing is written in stone when it comes to AI. It parameterized as much as possible, with only hardcoded static values being mathematical constants and physics formulas (but even these might be parameterized).

Everything else should be a changeable variable, dynamically altering based on weighting information from its environment. We are in a zone of "Artistic creativity and Intellect". Such AI software is resourceful, adaptive, and creative, with continually extending its knowledge base both by observation and experiment. Its ability to change and adapt is quick, and its own views and perspectives might differ as time goes on. Therefore, we need to categorize AI by the depth of its specialization and characteristics at least to 4 categories: Specialized, General, Hard, and Soft.

In IT typical techniques and tools include multiple approaches such as *Deep Learning*, Image – Sound – Emotion recognition, Content Creating bots, Automated Assistants, and all capabilities in first 4 Levels of

Automation – Quality Assurance, Full Automation Testing, Robotic Process Automation, and Machine Learning.

Between ML Mastery and the AI Kingdom are three important areas of software agents – Deep Learning, Reinforcement Learning and Automated Machine Learning. Therefore, all languages, tools, and techniques mentioned above in 4 Levels might be present.

L1 - Quality Assurance

In manufacturing and IT, Quality Assurance just as Test Engineering or Quality Control are jobs for professionals, who determines and creates processes that would best test a product under manufacturing. All related disciplines have a goal to assure that the product meets applicable specifications. Test engineers are responsible for determining the best way a test can be performed to achieve adequate test coverage (or ideally full test coverage).

Testing is divided into multiple categories, all aiming to find as many defects in a product under development as possible.

Continuous testing is a process of executing automated tests, for validating both functional and non-functional requirements, for the need of all requirements verification mentioned above.

This is where automation comes in, with a goal of *extending test coverage* and *leveraging release process* to production.

Testing types and techniques:

Functional requirements:

Exploratory – little or no preparation required, *freedom of approach*

White-box – programming skills required, *source code available*

Black-box – programming skills not required, *source code not available*

Unit – verify the functionality of a *specific section of code*

Component – focus on *data values passed between various units*

Integration – verify functionality and *interfaces between components*

Smoke – minimal attempt to *health check core functionalities*

Regression – *sets of test cases*, to find defects *after a major code change*

Non-functional requirements:

Performance – request and *response time measurements*

Load – sending big data in bytes, *stability under a workload*

Security – *access levels for different users* on all application layers

Stability – trying *invalid or unexpected inputs* and actions

Acceptance and **Release**:

Acceptance – *user or customer* testing if a *product meets specifications*

Alpha – *potential end users, operational testing*, still internal

Beta – *small audience* testing beta versions *released to the market*

L2 - Full Automation Testing

After acquiring Quality Assurance experience and perhaps ISTQB certifications (International Software Testing Qualifications Board), but still not being completely confident with all details which programming requires, the best way to move on is to become an Automation Tester and simply start *automating the most repetitive part* of your job – Regression tests.

In an ideal situation you join a team which develops new software, and you can build up automation test coverage from scratch same as development is progressing. But it's rarely the case. More likely is to *inherit some legacy code* either for development or testing and enhance it, and keep on with maintenance.

New software under development, and building test coverage from scratch

If your team is developing something new for customers, the best thing to do is to automate your tests *for each user story continually* as developers finishing it one after the other. Then you could combine steps, and create scenarios which make more sense to cover specifications. If QA Managers trust you enough and give you a free approach, this is your opportunity to study and *implement the newest frameworks* and technologies on the market. Keep in mind that you are not alone, and you should ask for help whenever you feel blocked.

Before starting to implement any tests, I suggest *appointing a couple of meetings* with QA Managers, Software Architects and Tech Lead from your team, and compare multiple articles of modern technologies and frameworks on the market. Combined with their expertise, your experience, and *fresh comparison from the market* you should be able to decide which ones to use to fit the technical suite of the team and its mission.

That's how we did it, and for our specific goals and purpose eventually, we had chosen Cucumber from many opensource frameworks, like TestNG, Serenity, Gauge,

Sahi, Cypress, Robot. There are many others, specific for mobile like Appium, or specific for browsers like Selenium, which you could integrate into Gauge or Cucumber.

Therefore, *communication about your specific goals and purposes is important*, and everyone should agree before you start putting together Automation tests or processes. That's why I suggest a couple of meetings, to decide about your specific approach.

Legacy code enhancement, and inheriting existing test suite

If your team inherits legacy code to enhance and maintain, there might be an already existing test suite which you will need to study. Some things might be good, and you can *learn from it by running and fixing tests*. Other parts of that test suite might be old and clumsy, where there is a chance for you to make improvements.

If your team inherits legacy code, but there is no test suite to verify the application, you can start to build the test coverage with *automating Regression tests*, which you need to run most often. Then continue with *Component (both API and UI)*, move along with *Integration* testing if there are other platforms or systems into which your application is integrated. And keep on extending with *Mobile* tests, *Security* tests or *Performance* tests if required.

Setting up your environment

Based on the programming languages you agreed upon with your team, you chose the appropriate IDE.
For Java, I suggest IntelliJ, for basic Python it would be PyCharm, but for Machine Learning purposes in Python, it would be Anaconda which includes more tools. For C# it's Microsoft Test Manager or Microsoft Visual Studio.

Integrated Development Environment (IDE) is a great helper. You can see all your project files in one place, you have distinguished colors for different syntax usages, but perhaps best of all are *keyboard shortcuts* (duplicating rows, or move them up and down), which really makes your job much faster and easier. You should search for them for your chosen IDE and learn them by using them.

Start with API

If I could give you one good hint about where to start, it would be API. Since development usually *starts with the back-end*, this is your first opportunity for automation right from the beginning.

Back-end developers beyond Unit testing also test their creation, before passing it to testers. To test raw data requests and responses (JSON or XML), they usually use Swagger, Postman, GraphiQL, or some Chrome extension like Restlet Client – REST API Testing.

You can play around with that by sending different request methods to certain endpoints they give you. HTTP Methods like POST, GET, PUT, DELETE on

https://testapplication.com/testapi/chapters/_search
(just an example) with a request body. Then you *verify status code* 200 and *response body*. There are many status codes in HTTP protocol, like 400 Bad Request, 401 Unauthorized, 403 Forbidden, 404 Not Found, or 500 Internal Server Error. Depending on what you are testing, the expected status code differs as well.

Eventually, you take those request and response sample data and create test steps for them in your IDE. But before that, you most likely need to integrate a certain framework in your IDE – it might be Cucumber, Gauge, TestNG or something similar.

When you created your first basic test, your goal is to *make it parameterized* not hardcoded, and be able to run it for different inputs vs. expected results. In such a way, each of your *methods will be reusable* for many step inputs and outputs.

Full Automation Testing approach example

A quick look at the application part under test and corresponding library or framework used to test it. Each step was programmed in Java either by me or already in a certain library, and for the top-level readable format I used Cucumber and annotations above programmed Java methods.

Collaboration tool — for BDD — Cucumber (or Gauge, or TestNG, or SahiPro)

API services — Cukes library for Cucumber (or any Rest client library)

UI functionality — Selenium WebDriver (or SahiPro, or Cypress)

UI „cosmetics" — Sikuli Image Recognition library

Mobile Responsive — Selenium mobile emulation (or add resolutions to Sahi)

Mobile Native – Appium with UI Automator

Performance – Step duration times in Cucumber report, and JMeter

Security – Combination of API and UI access levels

L3 - Robotic Process Automation

Digital Transformation

In this competitive world, we live in, employees are not the only ones who strive for survival. Company's goals of increasing productivity and efficiency have one main reason – to be the first who comes to market with their products and services. For this reason, we are entering a digital transformation era, which will make processes faster, more efficient, more precise, to the point, and so on. Among many approaches, I will introduce and compare two most likely to adopt mass market in close future. These are BPM - Business Process Management, and RPA – Robotic Process Automation.

BPM and RPA are different, but not competing approaches, and might work together in harmony. Both derive from company needs, which are revenue, efficiency, cost reduction, speed, and quality. To satisfy all these needs - to do more for less, implementing them in multiple company divisions seems to be the next logical step.

Definition of BPM

BPM is a strategic approach that aims for reshaping the organization's process management, and re-engineering process flows. It's defined in multiple steps which involve modeling, automation, execution, control, measurement and optimization of business processes. Popular BPM tools are Integrify, BP Logix, Process Maker.

Definition of RPA

RPA is a set of software technologies that enable employees to better focus on high priority tasks at hand. Low priority, routine, monotonous and repetitive tasks are given to software bots to complete. These software robots will be automated across Web, MS Office, emails, data management. On a basic level it can be configured even by non-technical persons, which does not require any programming. Popular RPA tools are Automation Anywhere, Blue Prism, Foxtrot, UiPath.

Comparison

BPM is a bit more disruptive way, which will intervene in the day-to-day running of the organization, and most likely reshape it at its core. A longer-term effort which could require dedicated technical resources and encompass a wide range of software technology.

RPA is a non-disruptive way, which can be built up alongside normal functioning of the organization. Rule-based, monotonous tasks, which does not require complex decision making can be given to software robots. Configuration on a basic level is easy and fairly non-technical. More automation and cross-platform might require more skillful resources.

Preparation for Transformation

Companies' productivity is crucial, however not every company is ready for digital transformation, and it's not easy to replace human potential. It requires lots of discussions, understanding, planning, skill set, and incremental buildup.

People who are best fit to buildup BPM or RPA have an insight for that specific company process, and a nice blend of Business Process Knowledge and Automation Testing. Such experts are obviously hard to find because these are two different types of roles.

So more likely there will be a team assembled, with *people who understand those processes* and understand *the need of the company to automate* those processes. A team consisting of automation experts, manager of the particular division under transformation, and tech lead.

The company needs *to have a plan* of what to do with the people whose jobs will be eventually automated. Should they keep persons who are experts in process knowledge, or persons who are experts in automation, or both?

Hopefully, they can keep both and not focusing purely on cost reduction. The best approach might be achieved *by extending their job descriptions and responsibilities*, meanwhile, BPM and RPA increase speed, quality and efficiency, and most importantly for the company - revenue.

L4 - Machine Learning Mastery

Machine Learning is a buzzword for more than a decade on the IT market, it came way before Robotic Process Automation, which is relatively a new field compared to ML. It's a programming technique for problem-solving without explicitly being programmed for each possible case of scenario, therefore it falls to automation subject with learning and predicting abilities. Put it to „The ART of Automation" context, we are talking about Machine Learning Mastery, which includes expertise in multiple types of Machine Learning, but especially Reinforcement Learning and AutoML – Automated Machine Learning.

There are many Machine Learning tools and APIs for developers. You can train an application which can recognize and differentiate an image of healthy grape leaves, from sick grape leaves which has some bacteria attacks (this is called Supervised learning). Or healthy lung x-ray images from lung cancer x-ray images (Supervised learning). But a different algorithm could predict house pricing, employee promotion, or come up with a specific number for salary raise for an employee (Regression or Forecasting). There's still a lot of potential with fascinating POCs - Proof of Concepts.

Types of Machine Learning

Machine Learning can be approached in several ways. How to decide which model or algorithm to use is important and depends on the problem we want to solve. It can be based on task, target, data, tradition, complexity or model.

Type of task: *Classification, Regression, Clustering, Episodic tasks, Continuous tasks*

Type of target: *Supervised, Unsupervised, Semi-Supervised, Reinforcement*

Tradition: *Naive Bayes, k-Nearest Neighbors, SVM, Decision Trees, Perceptron*

Complexity: *Artificial Neural Network or Convolutional, Deep Learning, AutoML*

Model: *27 types of Neural Networks or more*

Classification (Supervised)

Decides and chooses one decision among many by looking at experiences from the past. For example, decides between healthy grape leaves as category A, and sick grape leaves as category B. It's called *Supervised* because it requires data sets which are considered as correct (labeled set of data). This means that in a training dataset of flower/animal images each photo needs to be pre-labeled as roses/daisies or dogs/cats. When a new image is uploaded, the model compares it to the training examples to predict the correct label. There is a finite output, with or without a probability shown.

Regression / Forecasting (Supervised)

In a case of regression, ML agent looks at continuous data and makes a prediction of expected value by looking at multiple features. For example, giving it multiple parameters such as country, area, footage, population density, it can predict housing cost. It's more sophisticated and realistic since it could involve a big number of variables. *Supervised*, and requires data feed from different databases (reference points), which are considered as correct and true data. There is a finite output, an exact predicted number.

Clustering (Unsupervised)

Looks for patterns in observed events, and groups similar items into clusters. For example, finding clusters (nodes) based on similarities of nodes and strengthen those bonds which have lots of connections. For example, it could create a heat map of relationships between employees in a company, based on their communication frequency; skill set similarities, social life, age, and location. It's called *Unsupervised* because there is no correct labeling or true answer (there are no training datasets and no targets), which could be used for training. There are no finite outputs, categorization or prediction. It could be represented as many points (nodes) with different sizes and number of connections.

SVM

I have done myself a bit of Machine Learning for my college degree thesis, both for my bachelor's and master's degree. My thesis topic was "Image steganography with using QR codes and cryptography". You cannot find "Machine Learning" in its name, but I made a great deal of implementation first on my bachelor thesis "Steganalysis based on Binary Similarity Measures".

Image steganography is about hiding secret messages in pictures. In this case, they were QR codes evenly distributed at a layer of Least Significant Bits (LSB) of the picture, and those QR codes were encrypted with AES 128 ciphering method for more security. You couldn't recognize with plain sight if the image has a secret message in it.

Image steganalysis is about finding secret messages in pictures, with some probability. This is where Machine Learning takes place against different insertion algorithms such as F5, OutGuess, MB1, MB2.

In this case, I trained *a model with classifier, Support Vector Machine - SVM* of cover images suite (500 or more pictures with hidden images) against test images suite (500 or more pictures without hidden images).

This way a model was trained, into which I could upload an image and it was able to tell me with a probability if that image had a hidden secret message or not. But it's not able to extract, read, and evaluate the secret message. That would be a Level 4 Automation - Machine

Learning Mastery and would require multiple ML algorithms.

Reinforcement Learning

Such algorithms are based on rewards and punishments, depending if the software comes closer or further away from the preset goal. Rewards and punishments can be as simple as a counter variable. It resembles biological evolution, but RL evolution is incomparably and infinitely faster to gene mutation and natural selection. With such an approach you could teach a 3D model software humanoid from wriggling on the ground to stand up straight and start walking.

Because of these descriptions, RL is also referred to as Artificial Intelligence approach. Eventually, you could teach such AI to play video games, old and modern as well. These two examples already exist – both running software humanoids who learns and evolves in virtual environments (like evading obstacles) and AI learning while playing against itself, to perfect its algorithm.

More sophisticated Reinforcement Learning algorithms are implemented into dog robots, or humanoid robots to teach them in the same manner, as if it would be in a virtual environment or a video game.

AutoML (AML)

Automated Machine Learning has a huge benefit of speed, also it requires less manual analysis. It can go from Data Acquisition to Predictions with Full Automation, skipping through human time-consuming manual work of Data Exploration, Data Labeling, Feature Engineering, Model Selection, Model Training, Hyper-parameter Tuning.

Soon, automated end-to-end Machine Learning will be crucial for solving real-life problems in real-time. There is already a big need to speed up the process of data analysis required for ML algorithms. It's rightfully called an Artificial Intelligence- based solution, since once fully automated, it doesn't require any human attention, intervention, supervision or monitoring.

Deep Learning, Reinforcement Learning, and *Automated Machine Learning* are with one foot into the AI Kingdom. These are *half* of the ingredients to what I call in this book „The ART of Automation".

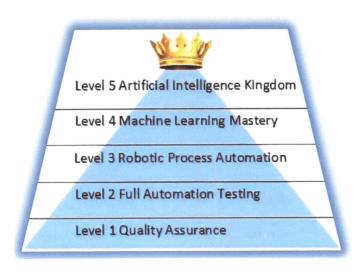

L5 - Artificial Intelligence Kingdom

Artificial Intelligence Kingdom – in this level programmers are required to be absolute experts. For perfecting a corporate process, manufacturing products or handling complaints, data analysis in real time – evaluation and response, everything automated and self-growing. We must differentiate between Narrow, Specialized ANI focused on a small niche market, and General, Full AGI focused on every aspect of life and knowledge. A different division is about an ability to adapt and change - Soft AI is more flexible, Hard AI is less flexible, more hardheaded and stubborn.

ANI – Artificial Narrow Intelligence (also called Weak AI, Specialized AI, Narrow or Applied AI)

ANI - Narrow AI is aiming to solve a small, specific set of problems. For example, Deep Blue from IBM in 1997 was aimed to beat than reigning chess master Garry Kasparov. Or AlphaGo from Google DeepMind in 2016, played and defeated in Seoul Go world champion Lee Sedol – and after that AlphaGo Artificial Intelligence received the highest Go grandmaster rank. Another IBM's Machine Learning system Watson was fed hundreds of images of artist Gaudi. Watson learned the features of Gaudi's work and then instructed human artists to create sculptures in his style. Watson BEAT is similar to generate music algorithms. In this category belongs Amazon's Alexa and Apple's Siri. They have limited pre-defined range of functions. Specialized or Weak AI can be just as dangerous as Generic AI, and fail in unpredictable ways. In 2010 there was a market crisis, a „flash crash" caused by AI trading algorithms.

AGI – Artificial General Intelligence (also called Strong AI, Full AI or General AI)

AGI - General AI would be like enhanced Alexa or Siri, with function capabilities in many different fields, operating *beyond* a pre-defined range of functions, adapting itself. If you've seen the movie „I, Robot" with Will Smith there was this all-knowing VIKI – an AI supercomputer. Designed and used by a robotic company, VIKI had a flaw being too concerned for humanity and therefore decided to wipe us out. Just like Skynet in Terminator. General AI could be described as *an expert in all combinations of Specialized Ais, able to react to all kinds of events.*

Hard AI (also called Hardheaded or Stubborn AI)

Hard AI could be headstrong and bad-tempered. For example, once it's learned and refined many Machine Learning algorithms let's say - with AutoML, and rewarded itself many thousand times with Reinforcement Learning, it's *hard to change its view*. For AI, a reward has an effect as dopamine for us humans. Hard AI could get *easily obsessed* with these rewards, just like humans could get addicted to sugar or drugs. If we have no control over it, this kind of AI is the most likely candidate for being destructive.

Soft AI (also called Flexible AI)

Soft AI is more flexible and carefully adaptable. Taking the same example, once it's learned and refined many Machine Learning algorithms with AutoML, it's very *conservative with its own rewarding system*. Reinforcement Learning still has a goal to perfect a certain behavior. But when it comes to actual decision making, it does it carefully and *considering the impact* it will make. It thinks more like a Chess Software, which thinks ahead dozens of steps and considers many situations.

What we know and what we don't know

To get a better sense of AI tricky parts, we need to divide it into two categories: what we know and what we don't know.

For ANI – Artificial Narrow Intelligence, we understand the specific problem and how to approach it. There are many successful achievements with ANI - specialized in chess, chatting, driving a car, playing video games. Some already implemented in our daily lives, like organic advertisements or chatbots, and some were shut down shortly after they were released to Production because it was a disaster.

For AGI – Artificial General Intelligence, it contains all problems possible, even if we understand most of them, we certainly don't know how to approach each one of them. We could compare AGI to „The Theory of Everything". There is a need to connect seemingly not connectable formulas of Machine Learning, and find the perfect mathematical functions or a single description. For both, we don't know how, yet.

To take it to the next level, 5th Level of Automation – Artificial Intelligence Kingdom software needs to be more creative and resourceful. It does not necessarily mean achieving AGI, because it contains every complex problem. Our focus is to apply ANI and understand the tricky parts of AGI.

Implementation

We have come to a point, where I can introduce you a quick start guide for automation approach. As an example, I'll use E-shop Management and ordering items online. There will be a short theoretical reminder and technical hints.

As I already mentioned, communication inside the team about your specific goals and purposes is important, and everyone should agree on languages, toolsets, and approaches before you start putting together Automation tests or processes. That's why I suggest a couple of meetings and comparing new tools and techniques from the market, to decide about your specific approach.

Full Automation Testing approach example

In this example, we will take a look at the application part under test and corresponding library or framework used to test it. Each step was programmed in Java either by me or already in a certain library (Cukes-rest, Selenium-API, Selenium-remote-driver).

I used Cucumber for a top-level collaboration tool because of its human-readable format. You can write your own steps in any format you prefer and in many optional languages (Chinese, Spanish, and more). For each corresponding test step, there is a programmed Java method below that with the step annotation.

Collaboration	–	Cucumber – BDD
API services	–	Cukes library for Cucumber
UI functionality	–	Selenium WebDriver
UI „cosmetics" library	–	Sikuli Image Recognition
UI mobile	–	Selenium mobile emulation
Performance times, Jmeter	–	Cucumber step duration
Security access levels	–	Combination of API and UI

All parameterized values such as users, passwords, URL, email are contained in an application properties file, which is unique for each environment (Dev, Test, QA, Prod), and looks like this:

```
app_admin      = TEST_1
app_user       = TEST_2
app_customer   = TEST_3
app_support    = TEST_4

app_password   = Pass1234
login_url      = https://login.app.com/processlogin.htm
app_url        = https://loginq.app.com/AppLogin/app/login.htm

api_url        = https://testapplication.com/testapi
base_url       = https://testapplication.com/
graphql_url    = https://testapplication.com/testapi/graphql
ui_url         = https://testapplication.com/testui
api_key        = '***abcd1234*****************************
user_email     = peter_muszka@testrapplication.com
app_proxy      = http://proxy.app.com:8080
app_build      = 1.0.0
```

Feature files in Cucumber

Test Steps in the following examples are written in *Gherkin* language, using Cucumber. All types of tests for API, UI, Mobile, „Cosmetics", etc. have a high-level format. It's best implemented for BDD – Behavior Driven Development, where behavior and specifications are clearly written. The First couple of Background steps and Scenario steps might seem complicated for non-technical persons, but they are especially necessary when we work with API, sending requests and expecting responses.

API Testing

```gherkin
@API @DEV @TEST @QA
Feature: API Create Order

  TC00001 BE - Create Order    US00001

  Background:
    Given App user "{{application.app_user}}" is authenticated using
"{{application.app_password}}" password at "{{application.login_url}}"
    Then let variable "sso_cookie" equal to cookie "SSOCookie" value
    Given baseUri is "{{application.api_url}}"
    And accept mediaType is JSON

  Scenario Outline: Create data and search with GraphQL
    Given cookie "SSOCookie" with value "{{sso_cookie}}"
    And content type is JSON
    And request body:

    """
    {
      "name": "<name>",
      "type": "<type>",
      "currency": "<currency>",
      "termOfDelivery": "<term>",
      "status": "<status>",
      "version": <version>,
      "orderItems":[

          "itemNumber": "<item1>",
          "count": <count1>


          "itemNumber": "<item2>",
          "count": <count2>


    }
    """

    When the client performs POST request on "/order"
    Then status code is 201
    And header "Location" contains "{{application.api_url}}/order/"
    And let variable "location" equal to header "Location" value
    And let variable "id" equal to value from response key "id"
    And let variable "id" equal to "{{id}}"

    #Search and save ID for Order
    Given cookie "SSOCookie" with value "{{sso_cookie}}"
    And the client performs GET request on "/order/{{id}}/synchronize"
    And status code is 200


    And I wait for process to finish

    Given cookie "SSOCookie" with value "{{sso_cookie}}"
    And content type is JSON
    And graphql request body:
    """
    orderedItems{
      queries: [

        type: TERM,
        match: EQUAL,
        field: "order",
        value: "{{id}}"


      page: 0,
      size: 1
```

```gherkin
    total
    elements {
        order
        supplier
        errors
    }
}
"""

When the client performs POST request on "{{application.graphql_url}}"
Then status code is 200
And response contains properties from json:

"""
"data": {
    "orderedItems": {
        "elements": [
            {
                "order": "{{id}}"
            }
        ]
    }
}
"""


#Search and save ID for Order
Given cookie "SSOCookie" with value "{{sso_cookie}}"
And content type is JSON
And graphql request body:
"""
headers {
    queries: [
        {
            type: TERM,
            match: EQUAL,
            field: "name",
            value: "<name>"
        }
    ],
    page: 0,
    size: 1,
    sort: [
        { property: "modifiedDate", direction: DESC},
    ]
}
{
    total
    elements {
        id
        name
        type
        currency
        termOfDelivery
        status
        version
        orderItems {
            itemNumber
            count
        }
    }
}
"""
When the client performs POST request on "{{application.graphql_url}}"
```

```gherkin
Then status code is 200
And response contains properties from json:

"""
"data": {
    "headers": {
        "elements": [

            "name": "<name>",
            "type": "<type>",
            "currency": "<currency>",
            "termOfDelivery": "<term>",
            "notes": null,
            "status": "<status>",
            "version": "<version>",
            "orderItems": [

                "itemNumber": "<item1>",
                "count": <count1>
            },
            {
                "itemNumber": "<item2>",
                "count": <count2>
            }
        ]

        }
    }
}
"""

When cookie "SSOCookie" with value "{{sso_cookie}}"
And the client performs DELETE request on "{{location}}"
Then status code is 200

When cookie "SSOCookie" with value "{{sso_cookie}}"
And the client performs GET request on "{{location}}"
Then status code is 404

And Update result in Agile System with API key "application.api_key" for usermail
"application.user_email" and proxy "application.app_proxy" for Test Case "TC00001" and
build "application.app_build" with verdict "Pass"

Examples:

| name  | type| currency| term | status    | item1| item2| count1| count2| version|
| Peter| NEW | USD     | ASAP | IN_ORDER  | 0012 | 0013 | 3     | 2     | 1      |
| Katie| NEW | EUR     | LATE | OUT_ORDER | 1111 | 1112 | 1     | 4     | 1      |
| Josh | ALT | BTC     | FAST | BOOKED    | 2222 | 2223 | 2     | 5     | 2      |
```

The above scenario will execute multiple times, depending on how many rows of data you enter to the "**Examples**" table at the bottom.

Most steps for such API testing you can find already implemented in Cukes-Rest library.

UI Testing

```
@UI @DEV @TEST @QA
Feature: QA End to End Customer

   End to End testing
   TC00002   Manage Eshop MVP: End To End Testing       US00002
   TC00003   Create New Order                           US00003
   TC00005   Order File Upload Update                   US00005
   TC00006   Order Detail Page - Add Item - FE          US00006
   TC00007   Order Detail Page - Edit Item - FE         US00007

   TC00011   Order Dashboard - Export to Excel- FE      US00011
   TC00012   Edit Order (Name, Notes, Items)            US00012
   TC00013   Order File Upload New (Detail) - FE        US00013

   TC00015   Icon is not displayed in the top left      DE0002
             of the capability
   TC00017   Light theme, text is invisible because     DE0004
             it has the same color as the background


   Scenario: Manage Eshop and Create Order list UI
   # Select all items, go to Eshop
      Given App user "{(application.app_customer)}" user is authenticated using
   "{(application.app_password)}" password at "{(application.login_url)}"
         Then let variable "sso_cookie" equal to cookie "SSOCookie" value
         Given baseUri is "{(application.base_url)}"
         And accept mediaType is JSON
         When cookie "SSOCookie" with value "{(sso_cookie)}"
         And content type is JSON
         And request body from file "features/Eshop_Management/api/payload/session.txt"
         When the client performs POST request on "eshop/rest/session"
         Then status code is 200
         Given Go to "application.ui_url"
         And Redirected to "application.app_url"

         Then I authenticate myself with App user "application.app_customer" and
   "application.app_password" password
         And Redirected to "application.ui_url"
         And I wait for loading indicator


      # Create Order UI
         And I verify icon for Eshop Management
         And I click on Create New Order
         And I click on Order Name and fill with "Esop Name" name
         And I click on Notes and fill with "order created" note
         And I verify icon for Eshop Management

         And I click on Add Items for Order
         And I click on Filter and search "PC components" keyword
         And I wait for loading indicator
         And I select list item
         And I click on "Next"
         And I click on Filtered Orders for searched Item number 1

         And I click on Save button
         And I wait for loading indicator
         And I click on Upload File
         And I select excel "My order.xlsx"

         And I click on Item Row number 2 and action Delete
         And I click on Delete button
         And I wait for loading indicator
         And I click on Item Row number 3 and action Delete
         And I click on Delete button
         And I wait for loading indicator

         And I click on Add New Item
         And I click on Item Number and fill "2222" number
```

71

```
And I click on Item Description and fill "NVidia graphic card" description
And I click on Item Quantity and fill "12" quantity
And I click on Save button
And I wait for loading indicator

And I click on Add New Item
And I click on Item Number and fill "0000" number
And I click on Item Description and fill """ '[~!@#$%]/\/^&*\()' """ description
And I click on Item Quantity and fill "0.5" quantity
And I click on Save button
And I wait for loading indicator

And I click on Item Row number 1 and action Edit
And I wait for loading indicator
And I click on Item Number and fill "12345" number
And I click on Item Description and fill "Item number changed" description
And I click on Item Quantity and fill "25" quantity
And I click on Save button
And I wait for loading indicator

And I click on Filter Order and search "0000" keyword
And I wait for loading indicator
And I click on Search All
And I wait for loading indicator

And I click on Item Row number 1 and action Edit
And I wait for loading indicator
And I click on Item Number and fill "0001" number
And I click on Item Description and fill "Item number changed" description
And I click on Item Quantity and fill "0.5" quantity
And I click on Save button
And I wait for loading indicator

And I go back to Eshop Management
And I wait for loading indicator
And I click on filter and search for "CUSTOMER SLOVAKIA 1" keyword
And I wait for loading indicator

And I click on Search Eshop Name
And I wait for loading indicator
And I click on Sticky Menu for Item number 1
And I click on Sticky Menu Export to Excel
And I wait for loading indicator
And I click on Sticky Menu for Item number 1
And I click on Sticky Menu View order
And I wait for loading indicator

And I click on Edit Order
And I click on Order Name and fill with "CUSTOMER SLOVAKIA S2" name
And I click on Notes and fill with "PC components" note
And I click on Delete Items
And I click on Add Items for Order
And I wait for loading indicator
And I click on Filter and search "CUSTOMER SLOVAKIA" keyword
And I wait for loading indicator
And I select list item
And I click on "Next"
And I click on Filtered Orders for searched Item number 1
And I wait for loading indicator
And I click on Save button
And I wait for loading indicator

And I verify image "eshop_management.JPG" or "eshop_management2.JPG"
And I click on Update button
And I click on Detail Sticky Menu
And I wait for loading indicator

And I click on Detail Sticky Menu Replace order
And I click on Upload button
And I select excel "CUSTOMER SLOVAKIA eshop short.xlsx"
And I wait for loading indicator

And I wait for loading indicator
```

```
And I go back to Eshop Management
And I click on filter and search for "CUSTOMER SLOVAKIA" keyword
And I wait for loading indicator

And I click on Search Order Name
And I wait for loading indicator
And I click on Sticky Menu for Item number 1
And I click on Sticky Menu Export to Excel
And I wait for loading indicator
And I click on Sticky Menu for Item number 1
And I click on Sticky Menu Delete
And I click on Delete button

And Update result in Agile System with API key "application.api_key" for usermail
"application.user_email" and proxy "application.app_proxy" for Test Case "TC00002" and
build "application.app_build" with verdict "Pass"
```

End to End test (E2E) above - for a *typical use case* or workflow. Usually, E2E Tests comes lately during development and *covers most of the application core features* (and verify fixed defects) in a single test.

Selenium WebDriver to locate elements, and make actions in the browser has easy straightforward methods like:

```
driver.manage().window().setSize(new Dimension(width, height));
element.click();
searchField.clear();
searchField.sendKeys(keyword);
```

or

```
driver.navigate().refresh();
driver.close();
```

Parameterized steps - to be smart, the best way is to define them in such way, that by changing just one or two values, you could select a specific row in a specific column, and verify a specific text. With steps like these:

```
And I verify text on Item Row number 11 and column value is "CUSTOMER · SLOVAKIA · 0011
IN-A"
And I verify text on Item Row number 12 and column value is "CUSTOMER · SLOVAKIA · 0012 ·
IN-B"
And I verify text on Item Row number 13 and column value is "CUSTOMER · SLOVAKIA · 0013 ·
IN-C"
And I verify text on Item Row number 14 and column value is "CUSTOMER · SLOVAKIA · 2222 ·
NVidia"
```

Implemented like this:

```
@Then("^I verify text on Item Row number (.*) and column (value)+is \"([^\"]*)\"$")
public void iVerifyTextForItem(Integer i, String col_Id, String elementItem) {
    String rowNumber = Integer.toString(i - 1);
    WebElement rowString = (driver.findElement(By.xpath("//div[@data-side='" +
rowNumber + "']//*[contains(@class,'" + col_Id + "')][2]//*")));
    System.out.println(rowString);
    clickableXpath("//div[@data-side='" + rowNumber + "']//*[contains(@class,'" +
col_Id + "') and (contains(string(),'" + elementItem + "'))]").isDisplayed();
    }
```

Mobile Testing

To choose the right tool or library, we first need to pick our approach to mobile testing. Are we testing a responsive Web application on a mobile device? Or is it a native mobile application on iOS or Android? Do we need to automate a process or game on a mobile device, or just the application / responsive web itself?

For responsive *Web application* testing on different mobile devices, I usually use Selenium WebDriver, with mobile emulation. In this example, I used chromedriver.exe, since I automated on Chrome and Windows, and mobile emulation adjusts the resolution for a specific device. For UI Testing, a general approach is to implement @Before and @After methods, and this is where you can program all settings before or after running each scenario.

```
@Before("@Samsung")
public void beforeSamsungScenario() {

    String currentDir = System.getProperty("user.dir");
    String chromeDriverLocation = currentDir + "/driver/chromedriver.exe";
    System.setProperty("webdriver.chrome.driver", chromeDriverLocation);

    Map<String, String> mobileEmulation = new HashMap<>();
    mobileEmulation.put("deviceName", "Galaxy S5");
```

```
ChromeOptions options = new ChromeOptions();
options.addArguments("disable-infobars");
options.setExperimentalOption("mobileEmulation", mobileEmulation);

driver = new ChromeDriver(options);
System.out.println("************* Samsung driver created *************");
}

@Before("@iPhone")
public void beforeIPhoneScenario() {

    String currentDir = System.getProperty("user.dir");
    String chromeDriverLocation = currentDir + "/driver/chromedriver.exe";
    System.setProperty("webdriver.chrome.driver", chromeDriverLocation);

    Map<String, String> mobileEmulation = new HashMap<>();
    mobileEmulation.put("deviceName", "iPhone 6/7/8");

    ChromeOptions options = new ChromeOptions();
    options.addArguments("disable-infobars");
    options.setExperimentalOption("mobileEmulation", mobileEmulation);

    driver = new ChromeDriver(options);
    System.out.println("************* iPhone driver created *************");
}
```

To implement launching for other devices just add more methods with corresponding names, and change the string "device".

In a statement mobileEmulation.put("deviceName", "device") for following:

"iPhone X", "iPhone 6/7/8 Plus", "iPad", "iPad Pro", and so on. You also need to implement @After methods, where you most importantly include the statement driver.quit(); to close Chrome.

Scenarios can be more or less the same as in your UI Test suite, just add a corresponding tag at the top of your feature file for a device you want to run the test for. If you would add @iPhone tag to the UI test mentioned above, it would run on such resolution and settings.

For native mobile application, I suggest Appium and UI Automator driver. For Android its perfect, but UI Automator for iOS is deprecated for newer versions, so you would need to use Xcode 7 or lower, and iOS simulators for version 9.3 or lower.

Locating elements - defining specific Web Elements is crucial for UI Automation. These Web Elements are fields, filters, buttons, menu options, checkboxes, rows, and columns of data.

```
@FindBy(css = "eshop-management > detail-action-bar > div.filter > div > input")
public WebElement searchOrder;

@FindBy(xpath = "//div[contains(@class,'--open')]//*[contains(text(),'All')]")
public WebElement searchAll;

@FindBy(xpath = "//div[contains(@class,'--open')]//*[contains(text(),'Notes')]")
public WebElement searchNotes;
```

Parameterized elements - defined for multiple uses. Like different combinations of row numbers, column numbers, and text to verify.

```
WebElement textVerify = (driver.findElement(By.xpath("//div[@data-sid='" + rowNumber +
"']//*[contains(@class,'" + col_Id + "') and (contains(string(),'" + elementItem +
"')))]")));
```

Locating elements on different platforms

Difference between Selenium and Appium is in elements, and how you locate them.

For Web – Selenium, best way is to use Developer Mode in Chrome, it opens by hitting F12 on Chrome. You can locate elements in such way, and trying your own CSS selectors or XPath.

There are 8 types of locators (selectors) in Selenium: ID, Class Name, Tag Name, Name, Link Text, Partial Link Text, CSS Selector, XPath.

For Native app – Appium, you usually use UI Automator as a helping tool to locate elements.

There are 5 types of locators (selectors) in Appium: ID, Class Name, Tag Name, Accessibility ID, XPath.

There are many hints on Stack Overflow how to combine element attributes with text, etc. I highly recommend you to learn writing your own XPath and CSS selectors, and ideally parametrize them for your test steps. They will be reusable.

For more detailed Mobile Testing approaches, I would suggest Aleksei Petrovski's Udemy course: „Mobile Automation: Appium Cucumber for Android & iOS + Jenkins". It was previously called „Test Automation with Appium, Cucumber and Ruby". This is for native mobile apps.

Image Recognition

Most applications going to mass market care about a preferably stunning, up-to-date User Interface. This requires detailed attention to "cosmetics". It includes icons, buttons, fonts, pop-up windows or modals, headers, or any images and charts. To test these, we will need Image Recognition.

In this example, I used Sikuli Image Recognition library, which I integrated into my UI tests. There are specific steps in the UI section which use Sikuli, these are:

```
And I verify icon for Eshop Management
And I verify image "eshop_management.JPG" or "eshop_management2.JPG"
```

Take a deeper look at the implementation in Java. In this case, we are verifying the application icon, and we *have insurance* in a try–catch form. It could be for a different resolution, browser interpretation or theme.

```
@Then("^I verify icon for Eshop Management$")
public void verifyIcon() throws FindFailed {
    String currentDir = System.getProperty("user.dir");
    Screen screen = new Screen();
    Pattern iconPattern = new Pattern(currentDir +
"\\src\\test\\resources\\features\\Eshop\\ui\\images\\icon.JPG");
    Pattern iconPattern2 = new Pattern(currentDir +
"\\src\\test\\resources\\features\\Eshop\\ui\\images\\icon2.JPG");

    try {
```

```
        assertTrue(screen.click(iconPattern) == 1);
    } catch (FindFailed e) {
        try {
            assertTrue(screen.click(iconPattern2) == 1);
        } catch (FindFailed i) {
            fail("Icon have not been displayed!");
        }
    }
}
```

For these two simple steps, the implementations are
almost exact. In the second case, the only difference is,
that as in input parameter you can specify two different
images, for example for Light Theme and Dark Theme.
The try – catch solution might look cheesy, but it actually
works for each theme.

```
@Then("^I verify image \"([^\"]*)\" or \"([^\"]*)\"$")
public void verifyImage(String image_path1, String image_path2) throws FindFailed {
    String currentDir = System.getProperty("user.dir");
    Screen screen = new Screen();
    Pattern image = new Pattern(currentDir +
"\\src\\test\\resources\\features\\Eshop\\ui\\images\\" + image_path1);
    Pattern image2 = new Pattern(currentDir +
"\\src\\test\\resources\\features\\Eshop\\ui\\images\\" + image_path2);
    try {
        assertTrue(screen.mouseMove(image) == 1);
    } catch (FindFailed e) {
        try {
            assertTrue(screen.mouseMove(image2) == 1);
        } catch (FindFailed i) {
            fail("Images have not been displayed!");
        }
    }
}
```

Two Java Classes above - Screen and Pattern are from a
sikulixapi.jar library and package org.sikuli.script;

Deep Image Recognition

For more advanced Image Recognition, I suggest Google API Cloud Vision – it's probably the most powerful. For more options, there is Amazon Rekognition (that's correct), IBM Image Detection. Or Clarifai, which lets you search images based on other images.

Performance Testing

Measuring request and response

Time duration measurements under a particular workload give us a good idea about these limits. With automated performance tests, you can get request and response durations, and easily verify if they getting better or worse over time. *Every application has limits.*

There is a certain number of request/user combination for a time period, which the application can handle. Otherwise, the request might timeout (408 Request Timeout, 504 Gateway Timeout), or the server goes down (503 Service Unavailable).

Integrating multiple libraries into Cucumber for testing API / UI / Mobile / Security will give you a benefit of a general performance idea. In Cucumber Report – Steps section you can sort steps by Occurrences, Duration, Average, Ratio. These are just basics, but it still counts if you don't want to dive into a deep Performance and Load testing yet.

Implementation	Occurrences	Duration	Average	Ratio
AppLogin.scrollBottom(String)	2	1m 23s 469ms	41s 734ms	100.00%
BeforeAfter.beforeIPhoneXScenario()	1	10s 750ms	10s 750ms	100.00%
AppLogin.uploadFile(String)	11	1m 44s 496ms	9s 499ms	100.00%
AppLogin.goTo(String)	26	4m 2s 090ms	9s 311ms	100.00%
AppLogin.ThenAuthenticate(String,String)	25	2m 41s 260ms	6s 450ms	100.00%
StepDefinitions.waitSomeTime(long)	96	4m 53s 589ms	3s 056ms	100.00%
AppLogin.switchTab(Integer)	4	12s 071ms	3s 017ms	100.00%
BeforeAfter.beforeSamsungScenario()	1	2s 630ms	2s 630ms	100.00%
BeforeAfter.beforeScenarioOI()	21	52s 116ms	2s 481ms	100.00%
BeforeAfter.beforeIPhonePlusScenario()	1	2s 373ms	2s 373ms	100.00%
BeforeAfter.beforeIPadScenario()	1	2s 312ms	2s 312ms	100.00%
AppLogin.clickInventoryname(String)	11	21s 901ms	1s 99ms	100.00%
whenSteps.perform_Http_Request(String,String)	240	6m 52s 987ms	1s 720ms	100.00%
TestResults.UpdateResult(String,String,String,String,String,String)	125	3m 13s 195ms	1s 545ms	100.00%
AppLogin.clickSideBar()	3	4s 429ms	1s 476ms	100.00%
AppLogin.scrollDetailBottom(Integer,String)	8	11s 613ms	1s 451ms	100.00%
BeforeAfter.afterScenarioSamsung()	1	1s 419ms	1s 419ms	100.00%
BeforeAfter.afterScenarioIPad()	1	1s 351ms	1s 351ms	100.00%
BeforeAfter.afterScenarioIPhoneX()	1	1s 244ms	1s 244ms	100.00%
AppLogin.clickSearchAll(String)	30	34s 384ms	1s 146ms	100.00%
AppLogin.closeBrowser()	2	2s 124ms	1s 062ms	100.00%
AuthenticationSteps.AppUserIsAuthenticatedUsingPasswordAt(String,String,String)	74	1m 17s 155ms	1s 042ms	100.00%
AppLogin.clickColumnPreferences()	13	12s 180ms	937ms	100.00%
AppLogin.verifyImage(String,String)	3	2s 536ms	845ms	100.00%
AppLogin.refreshBrowser()	5	4s 037ms	807ms	100.00%
AppLogin.verifyIcon()	15	10s 964ms	732ms	100.00%

If you see this in bad quality, I apologize. I tested multiple picture formats and resolutions, but after Amazon converting my EPUB to their own special AZW3 (KFX) format, it looked squashed in most cases.

Cucumber Report and Steps section, from a Test Suite containing API, UI, Mobile, and E2E tests. Most importantly it contains *test steps*, a number of *occurrences*, the accumulated *duration* for each step, their *average* duration, and Pass / Fail *results*.

84

Steps section here is sorted by Average step duration in descending order (longest at the top). What gives a good picture of performance is a method *perform_Http_Request*, which occurred 240 times, and on average it took 1 second and 720 milliseconds.

Methods like - upload file, export file, waiting for loading indicator, scrolling – also give a general idea about the application health.

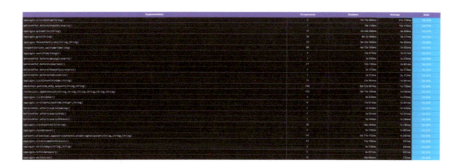

And eventually, you could adjust the colors of your report to match your application design, like in an example above.

Regarding performance, *in most cases*, requests and responses *should be faster*. But I also dealt with applications where anything under 2 minutes was considered great. So, the evaluation of results depends on requirements and usability. Results also can be affected by how old or new the integrated systems are, or the amount of data sent to the server to process (body size in bytes) over a period of time, or VPN connection.

Deep Performance measurements - I would suggest JMeter. It's easy to install and setup, you need to select a couple of menu items in JMeter to create a test.

Thread Group – number of **users** (threads) for which you run requests

Loop Count – number of **requests** for each user, like 5 or 20 etc.

Http Request Defaults – set **server** name or IP, such as testapplication.com

Http Cookie Manager – F12 on Chrome, then login and click Network, **Cookies**

Http Header Manager — F12 on Chrome, then login and click Network, **Headers**

Sampler Http request — set **endpoint**, such as /testapi/chapters/_search

Request Body — JSON or XML **request body**, list of items or parts

View Results Tree — Summary Report, Time Graph of Results

Security Testing

Security has great importance just like UI "cosmetics" or Performance. It can be approached both from API or UI perspective, and its main goal is to *verify access levels* for *different user roles*. The basic division would be ADMIN, VIEWER and EDITOR access levels for many user roles (might be 10 or more).

In below example, we have 3 roles: Administrator (ADMIN), User (VIEWER), Support (EDITOR).

User (VIEWER) *cannot* **C**reate, **U**pdate, **D**elete shopping orders – so receives 403 Forbidden status code for POST, PUT, DELETE request.

User (VIEWER) *can* **R**ead e-shop orders, and therefore receives 200 OK status code for GET request.

```
Scenario: Administrator
# Administrator WRITE access, creates initial order which other roles don't have
permission to delete
  Given App "{{application.app_admin}}" user is authenticated using
"{{application.app_password}}" password at "{{application.login_url}}"
  Then let variable "sso_cookie" equal to cookie "SSOCookie" value

  Given baseUri is "{{application.api_url}}"
  And accept mediaType is JSON

  Given cookie "SSOCookie" with value "{{sso_cookie}}"
  When the client performs GET request on "/users/me"
```

```gherkin
Then status code is 200
And response contains properties from json:
"""
{
    "username": "TEST_1",
    "authorities": [
        {
            "authority": "ADMIN"
        },
        {
            "authority": "EDITOR"
        }
    ],
    "appId": "TEST_1",
    "active": true,
    "firstName": "TEST",
    "lastName": "ADMIN",
    "email": "test.application@test.com",
    "groupName": "Administrator"
}
"""

# Create Order 201
Given cookie "SSOCookie" with value "{{sso_cookie}}"
And content type is JSON
And request body:
"""
{
    "name": "Testing Order for Access Level",
    "notes": "Automated Tests order",
    "order": "TEST",
    "items": [1111,2222]
}
"""
When the client performs POST request on "/orders"
Then status code is 201
And let variable "orderId" equal to value from response key "id"
And header "Location" contains "{{application.api_url}}/orders/"
And let variable "orderLocation" equal to header "Location" value

# Get Order
When cookie "SSOCookie" with value "{{sso_cookie}}"
And the client performs GET request on "{{orderLocation}}"
Then status code is 200

# Create a new item 201
Given cookie "SSOCookie" with value "{{sso_cookie}}"
And content type is JSON
And request body:
"""
{
    "description": "My New Item",
    "order": "{{orderId}}",
    "item": "2222",
    "quantity": "1",
    "rowNumber": "1"
}
"""
And let variable "orderId" equal to "{{orderId}}"
When the client performs POST request on "/items"
Then status code is 201

# Delete Order 201
When cookie "SSOCookie" with value "{{sso_cookie}}"
And the client performs DELETE request on "{{orderLocation}}"
Then status code is 200

Scenario: User
# User VIEWER access
Given App "{{application.app_user}}" user is authenticated using
"{{application.app_password}}" password at "{{application.login_url}}"
```

```gherkin
Then let variable "sso_cookie" equal to cookie "SSOCookie" value

Given baseUri is "{{application.api_url}}"
And accept mediaType is JSON


Given cookie "SSOCookie" with value "{{sso_cookie}}"
When the client performs GET request on "/users/me"
Then status code is 200
And response contains properties from json:
"""
{
  "username": "TEST_2",
  "authorities": [
    {
      "authority": "USER"
    },
    {
      "authority": "VIEWER"
    }
  ],
  "erpId": "TEST_2",
  "active": true,
  "firstName": "TEST",
  "lastName": "USER",
  "email": "test.application@test.com",
  "groupName": "User"
}
"""

# Create Order 403 Forbidden
Given cookie "SSOCookie" with value "{{sso_cookie}}"
And content type is JSON
And request body:
"""
{
  "name": "Testing Order for Access Level",
  "notes": "Automated Tests order",
  "order": "TEST",
  "items": [1111, 2222]
}
"""
When the client performs POST request on "/orders"
Then status code is 403


# Get order and save created date
When cookie "SSOCookie" with value "{{sso_cookie}}"
And the client performs GET request on "{{orderLocation}}"
Then status code is 200
And content type is JSON
And let variable "createdDate" equal to value from response key "createdDate"
And let variable "createdBy" equal to value from response key "createdBy"

# Create a new item 403 Forbidden
Given cookie "SSOCookie" with value "{{sso_cookie}}"
And content type is JSON
And request body:
"""
{
  "description": "My New Item",
  "order": "{{orderId}}",
  "item": "2222",
  "quantity": "1",
  "rowNumber": "1"
}
"""
And let variable "orderId" equal to "{{orderId}}"
When the client performs POST request on "/items"
Then status code is 403

# Delete order 403 Forbidden
```

90

```gherkin
    When cookie "SSOCookie" with value "{(sso_cookie)}"
    And the client performs DELETE request on "{(orderLocation)}"
    Then status code is 403

Scenario: Support
# Customer WRITE access
    Given App "{(application.app_support)}" user is authenticated using
"{(application.app_password)}" password at "{(application.login_url)}"
    Then let variable "sso_cookie" equal to cookie "SSOCookie" value

    Given baseUri is "{(application.api_url)}"
    And accept mediaType is JSON


    Given cookie "SSOCookie" with value "{(sso_cookie)}"
    When the client performs GET request on "/users/me"
    Then status code is 200

    # Create Order 201
    Given cookie "SSOCookie" with value "{(sso_cookie)}"
    And content type is JSON
    And request body:
    """
    {
      "name": "Testing Order for Access Level",
      "notes": "Automated Tests order",
      "order": "TEST",
      "items": [1111, 2222]
    }
    """
    When the client performs POST request on "/order"
    Then status code is 201
    And let variable "orderId2" equal to value from response key "id"
    And header "Location" contains "{(application.api_url)}/orders/"
    And let variable "orderLocation2" equal to header "Location" value


    # Get order
    When cookie "SSOCookie" with value "{(sso_cookie)}"
    And the client performs GET request on "{(orderLocation)}"
    Then status code is 200

    When cookie "SSOCookie" with value "{(sso_cookie)}"
    And the client performs GET request on "{(orderLocation2)}"
    Then status code is 200

    # Create a new item 201
    Given cookie "SSOCookie" with value "{(sso_cookie)}"
    And content type is JSON
    And request body:
    """
    {
      "description": "My New Item",
      "order": "{(orderId)}",
      "item": "0012",
      "quantity": "1",
      "rowNumber": "1"
    }
    """
    And let variable "orderId" equal to "{(orderId)}"
    When the client performs POST request on "/items"
    Then status code is 201


    Given cookie "SSOCookie" with value "{(sso_cookie)}"
    And content type is JSON
    And request body:
    """
    {
      "description": "My New Item",
      "order": "{(orderId)}",
      "itemNumber": "2222",
      "quantity": "1",
    }
    """
```

```
    "rowNumber": "1"
    }
    """
And let variable "orderId2" equal to "{{orderId}}"
When the client performs POST request on "/items"
Then status code is 201

# Delete Order 201
When cookie "SSOCookie" with value "{{sso_cookie}}"
And the client performs DELETE request on "{{orderLocation}}"
Then status code is 200

When cookie "SSOCookie" with value "{{sso_cookie}}"
And the client performs DELETE request on "{{orderLocation2}}"
Then status code is 200
```

Eventually, you could parameterize hardcoded values, and add more scenarios.

```
Examples:
| username| authority1| authority2| GETuser| POSTorder| POSTitem| DELETEorder|
| TEST_1  | ADMIN     | EDITOR    | 200    | 201      | 201     | 200        |
| TEST_2  | USER      | VIEWER    | 200    | 403      | 403     | 403        |
| TEST_3  | CUSTOMER  | VIEWER    | 403    | 403      | 201     | 403        |
| TEST_4  | SUPPORT   | VIEWER    | 200    | 201      | 201     | 201        |
```

These are just a few typical status codes, there are many more. Just to name a handful of important HTTP status codes: **200** OK, **201** Created, **400** Bad Request, **401** Unauthorized, **403** Forbidden, **404** Not Found, **503** Service Unavailable

Security Testing *in general* aims to prohibit any unauthorized access, and verify that confidential or sensitive data are protected. Specific UI elements might be confidential and keep their integrity and maintain functionality as specified.

Improvements

For Security testing described above, there might be *more edge cases, users, or request bodies* for which you could extend your security testing. And of course, similar scenarios needs to be implemented on UI side, because certain users are not allowed to see specific buttons, create new orders, add items to cart, or delete orders.

Therefore you might want to verify that a certain text (buttons) is, or is NOT present:

```
@And("^I verify text \"([^\"]*)\"$")
public void iVerifyText(String elementItem) {
    clickableXpath("//*[contains(text(),'" + elementItem + "')]").isDisplayed();
}

@And("^I verify text \"([^\"]*)\" is not present$")
public void iVerifyTextNotPresent(String elementItem) {
    try {
        WebElement noText = driver.findElement(By.xpath("//*[contains(text(),'" + elementItem + "')]"));
        fail("Text was displayed and it should not!");
    } catch (NoSuchElementException e) {
        assertTrue("Text was displayed", true);
    }
}
```

And you might want to implement Fluent Wait – dynamic waiting until a certain loading indicator disappears. In this example methods clickable XPath, clickable CSS, and clickable Element are working with dynamic waits.

93

```java
private WebElement clickableXpath(String xpath) {
    ExpectedCondition<WebElement> condition =
ExpectedConditions.elementToBeClickable(By.xpath(xpath));
    return fluentWait.until(condition);
}

private WebElement clickableCss(String css) {
    ExpectedCondition<WebElement> condition =
ExpectedConditions.elementToBeClickable(By.cssSelector(css));
    return fluentWait.until(condition);
}

private WebElement clickableElement(WebElement element) {
    ExpectedCondition<WebElement> condition = ExpectedConditions.visibilityOf(element);
    return fluentWait.until(condition);
}
```

Fluent Wait in this given example ensures polling (trying in intervals) every 300 milliseconds and ignoring „No Such Element" Exception and „Element Not Visible" Exception until loading is complete and elements appear. Timeout is after 20 seconds.

```java
public class AppLogin {

    private final HttpResponseFacade responseFacade;
    private GlobalWorldFacade world;
    public static ChromeDriver driver;
    public WebDriverWait wait;
    public FluentWait<ChromeDriver> fluentWait;

    @Inject
    public AppLogin(
            HttpResponseFacade responseFacade,
            GlobalWorldFacade world) {
        this.responseFacade = responseFacade;
        this.driver = BeforeAfter.getDriver();
        this.world = world;
        this.wait = new WebDriverWait(driver, 20, 300);
        this.fluentWait = new FluentWait<ChromeDriver>(driver)
            .withTimeout(30, TimeUnit.SECONDS)
            .pollingEvery(300, TimeUnit.MILLISECONDS)
            .ignoring(NoSuchElementException.class,
ElementNotVisibleException.class);
        PageFactory.initElements(driver, this);
    }
    .
    .
    .
}
```

Used like this:

```gherkin
And I wait for loading indicator
And I wait for "--open" to appear
And I wait for "spinner" to disappear
```

Implemented like this:

```
@Given(" I wait for \"{(\"#]*)\" to appears")
public void waitLoadingClass(String loading) {
    try {
    fluentWait.until(ExpectedConditions.visibilityOfElementLocated(By.xpath("//div[contains(@
class,'" + loading + "')]")));
    } catch (Exception ex) {
        assertThat(spinner.isDisplayed());
    }
}
```

Some of UI „cosmetics" could be limited for automation
from Image Recognition perspective (need to be verified
on many resolutions) or different each time (many
different colored themes). For these edge case scenarios
here is an easier approach with Selenium WebDriver,
which verifies if a certain element is displayed or not:

```
@Then("(View|Edit|Upload|Export|Delete) Is NOT displayed$")
public void isNotDisplayedItemOnSticky(String option) {
    try {
        WebElement menuItem =
(driver.findElement(By.xpath("//ul[contains(@class,'menu')]//*[contains(text(),'" +
option + "')]")));
        menuItem.isDisplayed();
        fail("Element should not have been displayed but it was!");
    } catch (NoSuchElementException e) {
    }
}

@Then("(View|Edit|Upload|Export|Delete) Is displayed$")
public void isDisplayedItemOnSticky(String option) {
    WebElement menuItem =
(driver.findElement(By.xpath("//ul[contains(@class,'menu')]//*[contains(text(),'" +
option + "')]")));
    menuItem.isDisplayed();
}
```

The pipe „|" divides optional inputs for the step. That
means Selenium will click on Web Element which you

define in Cucumber step, from specific pre-defined options.

You can store values from response keys in a variable, and use it later as in input for other steps. To store global variables I use here another benefit of Cukes library - Global World Facade. And you will need to import JSON Parser or create your own JSON Manager to be able to handle raw data from API.

```
@Then("^let variable \"(.+)\" equal to value from response key \"(.+)\"$")
public void var_assigned_from_response(String varName, String responseKey) {
    Map<String, String> stringStringMap =
jsonParser.parsePathToValueMap(responseFacade.response().getBody().print());
    System.out.println("\n");
    world.put(varName, stringStringMap.get(responseKey));
}
```

Sometimes you don't get the expected response right away, because there is a process running at the back-end, which needs to be finished. You could do a certain number of requests in a specific interval (polling) until you receive the Status you are waiting for.

As in this example of a *fully parameterized step* with 8 variables: type of request (POST, GET, PUT, DELETE), cookie name, cookie value, endpoint URL, intervals in seconds, number of requests, property key, property value.

```java
@Then("^do (.+) request with cookie \"(.+)\" and value \"(.+)\" on \"(.+)\" every (.+)
seconds for (.+) times until property \"(.+)\" has state \"(.+)\"$")
public void bodyContainsPathWithValue(String httpMethod, String cookie, String cvalue,
String url, Integer milliseconds, Integer times, String path, String value) throws
Throwable {
    boolean isResponseMatch = false;

    while (!isResponseMatch) {
        for (int i = 1; i <= times; i++) {
        {

            HttprequestFacade.cookie(cookie, cvalue);

            responseFacade.setResponsePrefix("");
            responseFacade.doRequest(httpMethod, url);

            System.out.println("\n");
            System.out.println("\n");

            Response response = this.responseFacade.response();
            String responseB = this.responseFacade.response().print();
            Boolean match = response.getBody().jsonPath().get(path).equals(value);

            if (!match) {
                Thread.sleep(milliseconds * 1000);
            } else {
                isResponseMatch = true;
                Assert.assertThat(response,
JsonMatchers.containsValueByPath(ResponseContentProvider.INSTANCE, this.getPath(path),
EqualToIgnoringTypeMatcher.equalToIgnoringType(value, this.world.getBoolean("case-
insensitive")))));
            }

        }
        }
    }
}
```

Used like this:

```
And do GET request with cookie "SSOCookie" and value "{(sso_cookie)}" on
"/orderedItems/synchronize/progress/{(process-id)}" every 10 seconds for 6 times until
property "message.status.state" has state "FINISHED"
```

Every tester on every project builds up necessary test coverage and makes improvements by him or herself, *as it best fits the needs.*

For example, I grow weary of dividing Java classes by POM (page object model) and instead I have each element locator and most implemented methods in a single class. So my test projects are less like a maze which requires a huge amount of investigation and searching through folders and subfolders.

In my case, tests are just as fast as if I would break down everything into small classes. But again, this might be different for you, depending on what your team prefers.

Robotic Process Automation

Digital Transformation with RPA

RPA is a non-disruptive way, which can be built up alongside the usual functioning of the organization. *Rule-based, monotonous tasks*, which doesn't require complex decision making could be given to software robots. These software robots will be automated across Web, MS Office, emails, Data management.

On a basic level, it enables non-technical configuration that does not require any programming. *Two most common RPA tools currently on the market: UiPath and Blue Prism – both are Drag-and-Drop and easy to pick up.*

This is how UiPath looks in Dark Mode. It has two basic scenario types: **Sequence and Flowchart**.

I created this simple **sequence**, so you could get familiar with the simplicity of the *drag-and-drop system*. On the left side, you can search, drag and drop activities to the middle and configure them on the right side.

For starters, just print out some text; verify a certain file and text within, logging results, and eventually sending an email. All this could be achieved without any programming, just by drag-and-dropping specific boxes and with the right configuration.

Flowcharts are easy to understand, especially for Business Process Analysts. Most people would prefer to describe and build automated processes with flowcharts. This might look more complex, but in fact, it's simple.

You could *store admin credentials in a secure location* in application properties, and your software robot will have access to it. Based on defined criteria, for each user in a file list – if a condition is met, the process at decision tree will continue with true steps, if not then with false steps.

In such way, you could build up an automated process, which would send out a specific email depending on gender, age, skill, birthday, name day, etc. only to persons which it relates to.

To refine some processes, you can write *additional scripts for example in Python*. You could input the code directly in the activity, or just drop RunScript activity and provide a file path to it.

It's still in Beta version, but UiPath will be able to *invoke your already existing Java codes* as well. For Python scripts, it's already working fine.

For more detailed overview and technical actions, both for companies and developers I would suggest Bryan Lamb's Udemy course: „Robotic Process Automation – RPA Overview", and „UiPath - Level 1 Robotic Process Automation", and „UiPath RPA - Level 2".

Machine Learning

To implement Machine Learning, we first need to decide which approach we will take. There are several ways how to decide which model or algorithm to use. It can be based on task, target, data, tradition, complexity or model.

Type of task: Classification, Regression, Clustering, Episodic tasks, Continuous tasks

Type of target: Supervised, Unsupervised, Semi-Supervised, Reinforcement

Tradition: Naive Bayes, k-Nearest Neighbors, SVM, Decision Trees, Perceptron

Complexity: Artificial Neural Network or Convolutional, Deep Learning, AutoML

Model: 27 types of Neural Networks or more

As you probably realized, there are a lot of options and paths to take. There also could be multiple different algorithms to solve the exact same problem. So which one you should choose? *Take into consideration the type of data you have at hand, and your target.* Based on that you can choose the right model.

Do you want to classify and label objects? Or predict a certain number? Or to have a software agent which would learn behaviors and have decisions?

Asking questions and based on your needs it could be either – classification, regression, or reinforcement (in this order for the three questions above).

Being able to pick the right Machine Learning approach and algorithm is what makes an ML Master. I will introduce 2 important types of Machine Learning approaches, regarding our "The ART of Automation" subject: RL and AutoML.

Neural Network algorithms which you will see below, the ones with a name „*Deep*" or „*Convolutional*" (or with many Hidden Cells), are the ones regarding *Deep Learning.*

With Deep Convolutional and Artificial Neural networks, AI companies were able to achieve big breakthroughs in the last years. For Neural Networks on JVM, I suggest library Eclipse Deeplearning4j.

I borrowed the image below with permission from Fjodor van Veen, and he asked me to mention **Asimov Institute**, which is an AI research company based in Utrecht, the Netherlands with a fantastic research team regarding Machine Learning, Neural Networks and Artificial Intelligence.

Shortly after I'll show you an example of how to *train a Neural Network* in a combination with *Reinforcement Learning* and *Deep Learning.*

On the next page are the *27 mentioned Neural Networks.*

○ Backfed Input Cell

● Input Cell

△ Noisy Input Cell

● Hidden Cell

◉ Probablistic Hidden Cell

△ Spiking Hidden Cell

● Output Cell

◉ Match Input Output Cell

● Recurrent Cell

◉ Memory Cell

△ Different Memory Cell

● Kernel

◯ Convolution or Pool

A mostly complete chart of

Neural Networks

©2016 Fjodor van Veen - asimovinstitute.org

Deep Feed Forward (DFF)

Perceptron (P)   Feed Forward (FF)   Radial Basis Network (RBF)

Recurrent Neural Network (RNN)   Long / Short Term Memory (LSTM)   Gated Recurrent Unit (GRU)

Auto Encoder (AE)   Variational AE (VAE)   Denoising AE (DAE)   Sparse AE (SAE)

Markov Chain (MC)   Hopfield Network (HN)   Boltzmann Machine (BM)   Restricted BM (RBM)   Deep Belief Network (DBN)

Deep Convolutional Network (DCN)   Deconvolutional Network (DN)   Deep Convolutional Inverse Graphics Network (DCIGN)

Generative Adversarial Network (GAN)   Liquid State Machine (LSM)   Extreme Learning Machine (ELM)   Echo State Network (ESN)

Deep Residual Network (DRN)   Kohonen Network (KN)   Support Vector Machine (SVM)   Neural Turing Machine (NTM)

Machine Learning Mastery – Reinforcement Learning

Reinforcement Learning does not deal with just tables of data or classifying and labeling samples. RL *agent* interacts with the real world or virtual *environment*, or simulation. Interaction means being in a *state* and taking *action*. And more importantly, it learns and evolves based on *rewards* as it continually tries out *actions* in its surroundings.

It's also a *big leap* from Supervised and Unsupervised learning. Continuous streams of data could come from sensors, cameras, microphones, GPS to characterize its *environment*. This is why Reinforcement Learning is with one foot in the AI Kingdom.

In its learning process, RL agent has a lifetime of development. At each step it decides what to do, and gets punished or rewarded, depending on if it gets closer or further away with its goals. It has similarities in psychology while testing mice behaviors and rewarding them with cheese if they successfully solve a maze.

Mouse in a **maze** is **deciding**

in a **position** which way to **turn**,

and for each (*successful)* **playthrough**

receives a **cheese**.

These are the seven important definitions in RL: **agent** (mouse), **environment** (maze), **policy** (decision), **state** (position), **action** (turn), **episode** (playthrough), **reward** (cheese).

Imagine a *Software Pilot* learning in simulated *environments*, and perfects itself by learning from thousands of situations before thrown into the real world. But it *never stops learning*. Would you consider such software as automation? Of course, that's why it's called Autopilot System. And sure, it could be developed in multiple ways. Also keep in mind that RL perfects itself as time goes on, after many playthroughs. So it will keep avoiding bad patterns, which will get him farther from its goals and punish the agent.

There are also types of tasks which are *repeating in cycles (Episodic)*, and types of tasks which are not repeating in cycles and therefore they *never end (Continuous)*. The main difference is, that with episodic tasks you have a terminal state, which signals the end of the episode. Like *checkmate* in chess or *three same symbols X or O* in a row, column or diagonal in tic-tac-toe.

Below is shown a process of *training a Neural Network in Python* for *two agents* playing tic-tac-toe. It's a combination of Reinforcement Learning and Deep Learning, using Markov Decision Process. It has a few pages so you can jump it through if you are more interested in the topic than actual implementation.

```
import random
import csv
import os
from pathlib import Path
from tabulate import tabulate
from abc import abstractmethod
import keras.layers as Kl
import keras.models as Km
```

```python
import numpy as np
import matplotlib.pyplot as plt


class TicTacToe():

    def __init__(self, player1, player2, exp1=1, exp2=1):
        self.state = '123456789'

        player1 = globals()[player1]
        self.player1 = player1(name='X', exploration_factor=exp1)
        player2 = globals()[player2]
        self.player2 = player2(name='O', exploration_factor=exp2)

        self.winner = None
        self.turn = 'X'
        self.player_turn = self.player1

        self.Xcount = 0
        self.Ocount = 0
        self.Tcount = 0
        self.all_count = 0

    def play_game(self):

        if isinstance(self.player1, QAgent):
            self.player1.exp_factor = 1
        if isinstance(self.player2, QAgent):
            self.player2.exp_factor = 1

        while self.winner is None:

            if type(self.player_turn) == Player:
                print(self.turn)
                self.print_game()

            self.state = self.play_move()
            self.game_winner()

            if self.winner is not None:
                break

        self.print_game()

    def play_to_learn(self, episodes):

        for i in range(episodes):
            # print('Episode number: ' + str(i))

            while self.winner is None:
                self.state = self.play_move(learn=True)
                self.game_winner()

                if self.winner is not None:
                    break

                self.state = self.play_move(learn=True)
                self.game_winner()

            # update last state
            self.state = self.play_move(learn=True)
            self.state = self.play_move(learn=True)
            # update winning state
            self.state = self.play_move(learn=True)
            self.state = self.play_move(learn=True)

            if i % 500 == 0:
                self.print_bar()
                print('--------------------')
                self.player1.print_value = True
            else:
                self.player1.print_value = False

            if i % 2000 == 0:
```

110

```python
                self.Xcount = 0
                self.Ocount = 0
                self.Tcount = 0

            self.all_count = i
            self.init_game()

        self.print_summary()
        self.player1.save_values()
        self.player2.save_values()

    def play_move(self, learn=False):

        if self.turn == 'X':
            if learn is True:
                new_state = self.player1.make_move_and_learn(self.state, self.winner)
            else:
                new_state = self.player1.make_move(self.state, self.winner)
            self.turn = 'O'
            self.player_turn = self.player2
        else:
            if learn is True:
                new_state = self.player2.make_move_and_learn(self.state, self.winner)
            else:
                new_state = self.player2.make_move(self.state, self.winner)
            self.turn = 'X'
            self.player_turn = self.player1
        return new_state

    def print_game(self):

        s = list(self.state)

        print('  {} | {} | {} '.format(s[0], s[1], s[2]))
        print('  -----------')
        print('  {} | {} | {} '.format(s[3], s[4], s[5]))
        print('  -----------')
        print('  {} | {} | {} '.format(s[6], s[7], s[8]))
        print('  -----------')
        print('  -----------')

    def game_winner(self):

        winner = [[0, 1, 2], [3, 4, 5], [6, 7, 8], [0, 3, 6], [1, 4, 7], [2, 5, 8], [0,
4, 8], [2, 4, 6]]
        for line in winner:
            s = self.state[line[0]] + self.state[line[1]] + self.state[line[2]]
            if s == 'XXX':
                self.winner = 'X'
                break
            elif s == 'OOO':
                self.winner = 'O'
                break
            elif not any(s.isnumeric() for s in list(self.state)):
                self.winner = 'No winner'
        self.check_winner()
        return self.winner

    def check_winner(self):

        if self.winner == 'X':
            self.Xcount += 1
            # print('The winner is X')
            # print('')
            # self.print_game()

        elif self.winner == 'O':
            self.Ocount += 1
            # print('The winner is O')
            # print('')
            # self.print_game()

        elif self.winner == 'No winner':
            self.Tcount += 1
```

111

```python
        # print('No winner')
        # print('')
        # self.print_game()

    def init_game(self):
        self.state = '123456789'
        self.winner = None
        self.turn = 'X'
        self.player_turn = self.player1

    def print_bar(self):

        plt.close()
        fig = plt.figure()
        ax1 = fig.add_subplot(2, 1, 1)
        ax2 = fig.add_subplot(2, 1, 2)

        x = ['X', 'Tie', 'O', 'Sum']
        a = self.Xcount
        b = self.Tcount
        c = self.Ocount
        d = self.all_count

        aprec = 100*a / (a + b + c + 1)
        bprec = 100*b / (a + b + c + 1)
        cprec = 100*c / (a + b + c + 1)

        ax1.clear()
        ax2.clear()
        bar1 = ax1.bar(x, [a, b, c, d])
        bar1[0].set_color('r')
        bar1[1].set_color('b')
        ax1.set_ylim((0, d + 100))
        plt.draw()

        bar2 = ax2.bar(x[0:3], [aprec, bprec, cprec])
        bar2[0].set_color('r')
        bar2[1].set_color('b')
        ax2.set_ylim((0, 100))

        for rect in bar2:
            height = rect.get_height()
            ax2.text(rect.get_x() + rect.get_width() / 2., 1.05 * height,
                     '%d' % int(height),
                     ha='center', va='bottom')
        plt.draw()

        plt.pause(0.05)

    def print_summary(self):
        a = ['X', self.Xcount, 100 * self.Xcount / (self.Xcount + self.Ocount + self.Tcount)]
        b = ['O', self.Ocount, 100 * self.Ocount / (self.Xcount + self.Ocount + self.Tcount)]
        c = ['Tie', self.Tcount, 100 * self.Tcount / (self.Xcount + self.Ocount + self.Tcount)]
        tab = tabulate([a, b, c], headers=['Player', 'num of wins', 'prec'])
        print(tab)

class Player():

    def __init__(self, tag, exploration_factor=1):
        self.tag = tag
        self.print_value = False
        self.exp_factor = exploration_factor

    def make_move(self, state, winner):
        idx = int(input('Choose move number: '))
        s = state[:idx-1] + self.tag + state[idx:]
        return s

class Agent(Player):
```

```python
def __init__(self, tag, exploration_factor=1):
    super().__init__(tag, exploration_factor)
    self.epsilon = 0.1
    self.alpha = 0.5
    self.prev_state = '123456789'
    self.state = None
    self.print_value = False

    if self.tag == 'X':
        self.op_tag = 'O'
    else:
        self.op_tag = 'X'

@abstractmethod
def calc_value(self, state):
    pass

@abstractmethod
def learn_state(self, state, winner):
    pass

def make_move(self, state, winner):

    self.state = state

    if winner is not None:
        new_state = state
        return new_state

    p = random.uniform(0, 1)
    if p < self.exp_factor:
        new_state = self.make_optimal_move(state)
    else:
        moves = [s for s, v in enumerate(state) if v.isnumeric()]
        idx = random.choice(moves)
        new_state = state[:idx] + self.tag + state[idx + 1:]

    return new_state

def make_move_and_learn(self, state, winner):

    self.learn_state(state, winner)

    return self.make_move(state, winner)

def make_optimal_move(self, state):
    moves = [s for s, v in enumerate(state) if v.isnumeric()]

    if len(moves) == 1:
        temp_state = state[:moves[0]] + self.tag + state[moves[0] + 1:]
        new_state = temp_state
        return new_state

    temp_state_list = []
    v = -float('Inf')

    for idx in moves:

        v_temp = []
        temp_state = state[:idx] + self.tag + state[idx + 1:]

        moves_op = [s for s, v in enumerate(temp_state) if v.isnumeric()]
        for idy in moves_op:
            temp_state_op = temp_state[:idy] + self.op_tag + temp_state[idy + 1:]
            v_temp.append(self.calc_value(temp_state_op))

        # deletes Nones
        v_temp = list(filter(None.__ne__, v_temp))

        if len(v_temp) != 0:
            v_temp = np.min(v_temp)
        else:
            # encourage exploration
            v_temp = 1
```

113

```python
            if v_temp > v:
                temp_state_list = [temp_state]
                v = v_temp
            elif v_temp == v:
                temp_state_list.append(temp_state)

        try:
            new_state = random.choice(temp_state_list)
        except ValueError:
            print('temp state:', temp_state_list)
            raise Exception('temp state empty')

        return new_state

    def reward(self, winner):
        if winner is self.tag:
            R = 1
        elif winner is None:
            R = 0
        elif winner == 'No winner':
            R = 0.5
        else:
            R = -1
        return R

class QAgent(Agent):

    def __init__(self, tag, exploration_factor=1):
        super().__init__(tag, exploration_factor)
        self.tag = tag
        self.values = dict()
        self.load_values()

    def learn_state(self, state, winner):

        if self.tag in state:
            if self.prev_state in self.values.keys():
                v_s = self.values[self.prev_state]
            else:
                v_s = int(0)

            R = self.reward(winner)

            if self.state in self.values.keys() and winner is None:
                v_s_tag = self.values[state]
            else:
                v_s_tag = int(0)

            self.values[self.prev_state] = v_s + self.alpha*(R + v_s_tag - v_s)

        self.prev_state = state

    def calc_value(self, state):
        if state in self.values.keys():
            return self.values[state]

    def load_values(self):
        s = 'values' + self.tag + '.csv'
        try:
            value_csv = csv.reader(open(s, 'r'))
            for row in value_csv:
                k, v = row
                self.values[k] = float(v)
        except:
            pass
        # print(self.values)

    def save_values(self):
        s = 'values' + self.tag + '.csv'
        try:
            os.remove(s)
        except:
            pass
```

```python
        a = csv.writer(open(s, 'a'))

        for v, k in self.values.items():
            a.writerow([v, k])


class DeepAgent(Agent):

    def __init__(self, tag, exploration_factor=1):
        super().__init__(tag, exploration_factor)
        self.tag = tag
        self.value_model = self.load_model()

    @staticmethod
    def state2array(state):

        num_state = []
        for s in state:
            if s == 'X':
                num_state.append(1)
            elif s == 'O':
                num_state.append(-1)
            else:
                num_state.append(0)
        num_state = np.array([num_state])
        return num_state

    def learn_state(self, state, winner):

        target = self.calc_target(state, winner)

        self.train_model(target, 10)

        self.prev_state = state

    def load_model(self):
        s = 'model_values' + self.tag + '.h5'
        model_file = Path(s)
        if model_file.is_file():
            model = Km.load_model(s)
            print('load model: ' + s)
        else:
            print('new model')
            model = Km.Sequential()
            model.add(Kl.Dense(18, activation='relu', input_dim=9))
            model.add(Kl.Dense(18, activation='relu'))
            model.add(Kl.Dense(1, activation='linear'))
            model.compile(optimizer='adam', loss='mean_absolute_error',
                          metrics=['accuracy'])

        model.summary()
        return model

    def calc_value(self, state):
        return self.value_model.predict(self.state2array(state))

    def calc_target(self, state, winner):

        if self.tag in state:

            v_s = self.calc_value(self.prev_state)

            R = self.reward(winner)

            if winner is None:
                v_s_tag = self.calc_value(state)
            else:
                v_s_tag = 0

            target = np.array(v_s + self.alpha * (R + v_s_tag - v_s))

            return target

    def train_model(self, target, epochs):
```

115

```
        X_train = self.state2array(self.prev_state)

        if target is not None:
            self.value_model.fit(X_train, target,    =epochs,    =0)

    def save_values(self):
        s = 'model_values' + self.tag + '.h5'
        try:
            os.remove(s)
        except:
            pass
        self.value_model.save(s)

def check_player():
    # print('QAgent X 1 and QAgent 1 0')
    # game = TicTacToe('QAgent', 'QAgent', 1, 0)
    # game.play_to_learn(1000)
    # print('DeepAgent X 0.8 and DeepAgent 0.8')
    # game = TicTacToe('DeepAgent', 'DeepAgent', 0.8, 0.8)
    # game.play_to_learn(30000)
    print('DeepAgent X 0 and QAgent 1, 0')
    game = TicTacToe('Player', 'DeepAgent', 0.8, 0.8)
    game.play_game()

check_player()
```

In the above example, *Two Agents X and O are learning* to play tic-tac-toe *against each other*.

If you are more curious, you could download the associated files, import it to *free **Anaconda,*** where it's easy to include packages like *NumPy*, *TensorFlow* and many more. There is also a new, combined IDE on the market called ***PyCharm for Anaconda***. Eventually you can *train the model yourself* and challenge the agents.

I used the Python code above with permission from Gilad Wisney. You can find it with all included files and more information in his article, called "Reinforcement Learning and Deep Reinforcement Learning with Tic Tac Toe" on *https://towardsdatascience.com*.

It's a very small reminder of AlphaGo from Google DeepMind which played and defeated Go world champion Lee Sedol in 2016. Since **Go** is played on a grid of 19x19 with two pieces, and tic-tac-toe has only squares 3x3 with two symbols and just 1 rule, tic-tac-toe requires much less computation with several orders of magnitude.

Go looks simple, but it is more difficult to solve than a chess game, which has less than half of its size, 8x8. Despite the simple look of two stones of Go (black and white), it is considered to require *deeper strategy and qualitative principles* than chess, which has 6 different types of pieces and many rules.

Other important aspects are *delayed rewards (values)*, which forces the agent to rethink its previous episodes and be able to plan a future strategy. In this quick start guide, I will spare you from deep mathematical formulas, but they are crucial for all implementations of Machine Learning algorithms.

For Reinforcement Learning on JVM, I suggest Eclipse RL4J library, and for Python definitely NumPy, SciPy, RLPy and definitely Keras, which includes TensorFlow.

For more detailed dive-in to AI and RL, I would suggest Lazy Programmer's Udemy course: „Artificial Intelligence: Reinforcement Learning in Python". Prepare yourself, there will be a huge amount of math formulas, as with ML in general.

Machine Learning Mastery – AutoML (AML)

If you are *frustrated* with the complexity of Machine Learning, *AutoML* might be the solution for you. It answers all these questions like: Should I label and transform input data? What ML algorithm would be best for me – SVM, logistic regression, decision trees? What parameter values should they use?

The <u>accuracy</u> of Machine Learning will be determined by these decisions. Fortunately, Automated Machine Learning solves them, by the combination of data preprocessing, choosing the right learning algorithms, and setting hyperparameters for you.

Certain tasks can be *automated* in machine learning, like hyperparameter search and tuning with Eclipse Arbiter library. Now try to imagine a thousand dimensions of data features, across which an automated software could see just the right functions to separate your data, and select the most relevant features – such *program chooses* the *right algorithm*, or makes a Model Selection, and chooses the right features, a.k.a. Feature Selection.

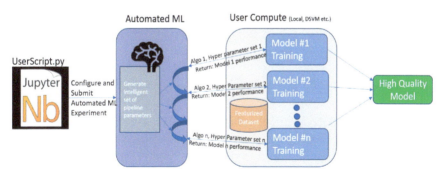

Image concept from Azure Machine Learning contributors

AutoML – time consuming manual work of Data Exploration, Feature Engineering, Model Selection, Model Training, Hyper-Parameter Tuning – it's all automated, and jumps right to Predictions.

Imagine building up Full Automation in a corporation for processes on RPA level, which means *handling thousands of daily basis tasks for hundreds of employees*. Now, imagine bringing many Machine Learning layers into these processes. It would be a long and painful journey, without such *enhancement as AutoML*.

With many processes automated, and improved with AutoML, such software bot would be *able to differentiate* between many voices, faces, emotions, ideas, documents, requests. It would be able to *make predictions* such as promotions, salary raise, suggest courses, events, and set up meetings. „A Beginner's Guide to Automated Machine Learning & AI" on https://skymind.ai/wiki/automl-automated-machine-learning-ai

Artificial Intelligence

Now, we come to the highest or uppermost point of our journey. Even here we need to divide AI into two categories: what we know, and what we don't know.

ANI – Artificial Narrow Intelligence, we understand the specific problem and how to approach it. There are many successful achievements with ANI - specialized in chess, chatting, driving a car, playing video games. Some already implemented in our daily lives, like organic advertisements, chatbots or trading bots. Some were shut down immediately after they were released to the market because it get quickly out of control.

A bit *scary*, since such AI can have strong male inclination regarding human resources (as Amazon learned in 2015 with their hiring bot), have sexist and Neo-Nazi views on social media (as Microsoft learned with their chatbot in 2016). Self-driving cars and taxis had some downfall and accidents as well. There is huge progress in the field of

ANI, so we have to be really careful to don't create software which gets out of our control.

On a *positive* side, we have already witnessed powerful ANIs, like Deep Blue from IBM in 1997, AlphaGo from Google DeepMind In 2016. And I'm sure we can expect in near future perfected versions of Amazon's Alexa and Apple's Siri, enhanced self-driving cars and many more. Chinese electric car company NIO has its own Artificial Intelligence Assistant called Nomi.

An *RL agent learning* to play tic-tac-toe in a strategic way was a *small taste of Artificial Narrow Intelligence.*

AGI – Artificial General Intelligence, since it *contains all problems* possible, even if we understand most of them, we certainly don't know how to approach each one of them. *We could compare AGI to „The Theory of Everything".* There is a need to connect seemingly not connectable formulas of Machine Learning and find the perfect mathematical functions, or a single formula. For both, we don't know exactly how, yet.

Reinforcement Learning combined with **Automated Machine Learning** gives as *real-time processing leverage* of automated end-to-end applied machine learning to *real-world problems*. With continuous streams of data from the environment (through sensors, cameras, microphones, GPS), it can learn and evolve rapidly. It will be rewarded for learning, speed, quality, precision, winning, usefulness, correct predictions, and so on. But most importantly, it should be rewarded for subtle and positive human interactions, such as sharing, bonding, laughter.

Rewards and punishments are based on feedback, which AI receives with its *interactions with the environment*. It will either perfect its behavior in a certain direction or try something different. AI or RL agent always *evolves towards certain goals*. For example giving satisfactory answers, winning competitions, find the right balance between usefulness, obedience, and entertainment – which is user specific. Since it only learns in the **process of trying – failing – improvement**, there are many mistakes made in the course of developing its intelligence.

An absolute extreme example of AGI would be from my favorite movie trilogy – The Matrix. If you would watch these movies a dozen times, I think you would still find something new what you have missed before.

The Matrix is an *AI-generated* simulated world, created by The Architect software – which is likely a Hard and General AI behind the face of Deus Ex Machina, an evil spiky machine which appeared at the end of Matrix Revolutions. The Architect (AGI) *created multiple versions* of Matrix, such as Paradise Matrix or Nightmare Matrix, to create the most *acceptable version to enslave humans.* Perhaps even more interesting AI's are Agent Smith and The Oracle. Both had *expressive goals and predicting abilities.*

Consider this significant list of Artificial Intelligence in the Matrix:

Deus Ex Machina (*Central Interface*, the most powerful machine)

The Architect (*AI software-generator* and chief administrator of the system)

Agent Smith (*RL Agent, Gatekeeper, exile sentient program and virus*), A. Brown, A. Jones, A. Thompson...

The Oracle (*supporting program* to interpret human psyche and intuitions, by making "*cookies*")

Seraph (*security software* protecting The Oracle)

Merovingian (*trafficker of information with exiles*)

Twins (*exile phantom programs*)

Cain and Abel (*exile old version programs* in the form of werewolves and vampires)

Trainman (*exile smuggler* and *connector* between The Matrix and the real world)

The Keymaker (*decryption program* designed to *open hidden doors*, especially to the *Source*)

All coming together

Imagine *building up Full Automation* corporate processes on RPA level, which means handling hundreds of daily basis tasks for all employees and customers. Now, imagine bringing many *Machine Learning layers* into these processes, for example with *AutoML* – Automated Machine Learning. Such software bot would be able to differentiate between many messages, requests, voices, faces, emotions, ideas, and documents.

Automated Machine Learning has a huge benefit in speed. It can go from Data Acquisition to Predictions in a blink of an eye, skipping through human time-consuming manual work of Data Exploration, Feature Engineering, Model Selection, Model Training, Hyper-Parameter Tuning – it's all automated, and jumps right to Predictions.

Combined with Reinforcement Learning, where a Software Robot learns and evolves during its interactions in any kind of environment, gets as really close to achieving AGI. To enhance our prototype of Artificial General Intelligence, we need to parameterize any left hardcoded values. Our created "Artistic Intellect" should dynamically alter its knowledge base, by weighting information it receives. This way we give it the ability to change and adapt its own views and perspectives.

Automated processes have *certain orders* in its step execution. To take it to a higher level, our software bots will need to be able to change step execution order, step priority, step values, extending steps, try different approaches. It's like a software bot evolution – but compared to biological evolution, gene mutation and natural selection its incomparably and infinitely faster. Especially if you include Reinforcement Learning, where you reward the software for combined speed and quality solutions, and it runs and tries many thousand approaches in a matter of minutes or hours. For biological evolution, it can take millions of years, while AI could achieve the same amount of experience in minutes thanks to processing power.

Knowing all this, I want to introduce you a different perspective to 5 Levels of Automation. Its knowledge, skillset, and experience-based view. It shows how much insight each higher level of automation requires. If you want to move your automation to a higher level, prepare yourself that there are more skills, tools, programming languages, mathematical models, algorithms, insights you have to acquire. And beyond that, you will learn to be patient, resourceful, problem-solving.

We must keep many things in mind, as we move through different levels of automation and zones:

Rule-Based Automation (Bots) (Levels 1-3)

Learning and Differentiation (Agents) (Level 4)

ARTistic Creativity and Intellect (AGI) (Level 5)

Each higher level of automation brings *more social concerns*, which needs to be solved alongside its implementation and mass adoption. These are mostly fears of losing jobs, devaluation on market, disrupting the market, too much control, or losing control, software learning bad views too quickly.

Many discussions and preparations, monitoring and testing are required to come up with right solutions, and don't cause any harm, confusion or chaos. *This is where Software and Human collaboration takes a crucial place*, despite our goal of Full Automation or Full AGI.

This is „**The ART of Automation**" in its true form –
achieving high levels of automation agents, but at the
same time *keeping the human qualities* and aspects to it.

Conclusion

For a final word, keep in mind:

To be a Full Automation Tester means that as time goes by you learn a lot. You learn a lot about back-end, databases, API services, front-end, security, mobile devices, performance, integration, understanding, and testing applications end-to-end.

At the same time, you will learn to effectively communicate with your team members and clients, your nerves will be stronger, and you will acquire a bunch of valuable qualities, just as your automation tests. Such as problem-solving, being more adaptive, resourceful, team spirit, dedicated, and patient. And just as your implementation, you will become more flexible and extendible.

To be more competitive with advantage, companies are looking for smart ways to automate processes and daily basis tasks. This is where Robotic Process Automation will play a big role in the upcoming years. It might be divided into two short development phases, Assisted RPA 1.0 and Unassisted RPA 2.0.

Multiple Machine Learning algorithms to recognize faces – voices – emotions – documents – requests will be put on top of RPA to bring it to the next level. Such Machine Learning algorithms could be created with software automation – where Automated Machine Learning development could play a crucial role.

Daily life in corporate should be less bureaucratic, and companies with a focus to achieve competitive advantage will need to combine precision, faster delivery, and top quality. Before implementing any level of automation, *many discussions and preparations, monitoring and testing are required* to come up with the right solutions and avoid any harm, confusion or chaos.

With all technical leverages which we will eventually achieve, we need to *take to special consideration the human aspects*. Social concerns should be resolved, and new values brought to surface with *Human - Software* collaboration. Such an approach will create precious and protective values, despite our goal of Full Automation or Full AGI.

A *harmonious balance* of *personal qualities*, collaborating with *high levels of automation* is „**The ART of Automation**".

My IT Background

As a kid growing up in the 90's I've always been astonished and enthusiastic about computers. My father had and still has a small computer business. I remember when we were kids with my brother Patrik, I was about 10 and our father brought home all those separated components and showed and described them for us. Fantastic times.

When it was up and running, we started installing the OS, setting up the environment and about a dozen desktop applications.

I continued with my IT journey in industrial high school, studying electrical engineering and computer science. My father opened 2 new stores (from which only 1 survived), and I spent some time there doing service for customers.

Me on the left at 13, and my brother on the right at 12, putting computers together in the kitchen on a casual Sunday morning

Next logical step for me was to study at Technical University with a focus on informatics, telecommunications, network technologies, and cryptography. My thesis both for my bachelor's and master's degree involved a great deal about multimedia security and machine learning.

My Bachelor's thesis - Image steganalysis based on Binary Similarity Measures (finding secret messages)

My Master's thesis - Image steganography using QR codes and cryptography (hiding secret messages)

While still in college, I had multiple part-time jobs and worked as an IT Assistant as well.

At the end of 2015, right after I came back from the US after a prolonged work and travel summer, I joined Global Logic IT Software Company in Kosice (Slovakia) - first part-time than full time, while still studying in college.

First, I worked as a Manual Tester for almost a year, on multiple medical projects. We were creating a website and software for Diabetes clinics and doctors, through which they could upload data from insulin pumps and glucose monitoring devices. Eventually, diabetes doctors were able to generate 30-page long medical reports full of charts, tables, diagrams, historical data, and prescription.

As a testing team, our job was to verify that all customer requirements were met, and there are no defects and bugs in the software.

The problem was that we had to verify all functionalities on multiple devices/ OS/ browser combinations. There were PC's, MacBooks, Tablets, Mobiles, Windows 7/8/8.1/10, iOS 8/9/10/11 and of course many versions of Chrome, Mozilla, IE, Edge, and Safari.

After doing the same thing repeatedly manually, every one of us went nuts at the end of the day. And imagine that there was a Dry Run for a couple of weeks, a developing period through which our job was to filter out most defects possible. Right after that was a Formal Run, an acceptance phase in which we basically did the same thing, but each combination of test cases printed out on paper, and doing the same thing in more bureaucratic fashion.

There were thousands of pages stacked and marked on multiple huge piles. It was a huge waste, which went on at least once every other month.

In my spare time at work, I always tried out new things, learned to code or programmed some of my ideas. There was a version of chess 4 versus 4 in Python which I programmed, or later a Cashflow Scanner in Android.

So, after a time I acquired some skills and moved to semi-automation, where I was testing raw data in those glucose monitoring devices. It required a lot of manual inputs as well, so I'm sure I would eventually automate the process step by step, to move it from semi-automation to full automation.

After a couple of months, there was a rundown on these medical projects, and we had to switch to personalized digital media project – automated advertisements, promotions, coupons. Those systems and software were so old and clumsy, that I've got enough after four months.

But meanwhile I learned a lot about automation and BDD - Behavior Driven Development. Especially I learned a lot from my senior colleague, who automated tests in a web browser, Cyril Jusko – Big Kudos.

After four months of working with really old systems and environments, I switched to a different company at the beginning of 2018 for a fresh start. In Ness, a new company for me, they had so much trust in me, which I'm thankful for, that after several discussions and meetings they gave me free hands to automate as much as I could and however I want.

That was really a fresh, kick-start for me, working on Inventory Optimization, handling hundreds of RSPL (Recommended Service Parts List) and eventually e-commerce. For me, a new company, project, team members, and also up-to-date code and frameworks were like thriving in heaven. So, I went on by myself as a tester for seven developers, and right from the start automated the test for each little user story and task which developers were creating.

Obviously, I did receive help from my teammates and more experienced architects. That's how we chose the right frameworks right from the beginning. We set up a meeting: QA managers with more than a decade of expertise in testing, a software architect with valuable insights, and me with my automation experience. We searched for some articles related to our mission, something which might solve our set of problems in the long term. A flexible, extendible approach with readable format included.

That's how we choose Cucumber as a top-level framework, because of its plasticity as a collaboration tool. Since then I'm scripting in human readable sentences, and then program the logic below it through annotations and optional language. As a tester, you should preferably use what your teammates use, so if mostly Java then Java, if Python then Python, etc.

So that was the idea. As time went by, I integrated every necessary framework which I needed to test certain functionalities. We still have Cukes library for API testing, which covers REST and GraphQL requests and responses, status codes, etc.

For UI testing I still use Selenium WebDriver for browser automation, with which I already had a lot of experience. Some might prefer Cypress or Sahi, but you should always check for integration options, you might need to extend your automation later.

With Selenium, it's also possible to test responsive Web apps on Mobile and Tablet. I simply run the same UI test suites and just programmed mobile emulation setup for them.

The last, but still significant integration was for UI "cosmetics" testing. Such as icons, buttons, colors, headers.

For that, I use Sikuli library, based on Image Recognition. You could snip and crop certain images from design, wireframe, locally deployed UI or from already working code deployed on Dev environment, and use that as a test image. The test will verify in those steps if such images are present in any of your screens.

So, with this little set of frameworks, below that the functionalities programmed in Java, I could automate 100% of tests for all user stories, for three related products.

All in all, for one product's initial release there were about 32 feature files in human- readable format, with 66 scenarios and more than 3000 steps. Every time there was a new deploy, release to Dev / Test / QA / Prod environment I rerun my test cases. It generated a nice, colorful report with basic performance information as well.

The best thing is, that in half an hour it covers the whole application and verifies functionalities in-and-out, back-and-forth. I could take a break for a couple of minutes, perhaps lie back in my multicolored bean bag next to our huge ficus and relax. When it's done, I carefully evaluate the results and either fix tests, extend them, or set up a report for the team.

About the Author

Peter Muszka is a Full Automation Tester at Ness KDC, focusing on Quality Assurance for Web applications under development and during release to Production. Studied Computer Science, Telecommunications and Networking Technologies.

Nowadays studies Robotic Process Automation approaches and going back to Machine Learning. Especially Reinforcement Learning and Automated Machine Learning - to find an ideal blend of all these software leverages to create more sophisticated, automated enhancements.

Follow me:

https://www.linkedin.com/in/peter-muszka

https://www.facebook.com/peter.d.muszka

Send me an e-mail:

pe.muszka@gmail.com

Acknowledgements

For my parents Peter and Anna, who always gave me an infinite amount of support and love for whatever I choose to chase. Thank you father for sharing your IT and computer skills, and for giving me support in my life. And thanks mom for your love and a great amount of care. I Love you, Mom & Dad.

My brother Patrik Muszka deserves a SPECIAL Acknowledgement for a VERY SPECIAL birthday gift, which is the beautiful cover of this book, and all the extra designs and promotions. Thank you that you found the time to create this awesome gift in the short amount of your time between traveling the world, video editing, your studies, work, and crazy social life. Love you.

Many thanks to IT companies who provided me their trust, equipment, tools or insights during my job: to Global Logic, Ness and Solar Turbines. Special thanks to Silvia Stevlikova and Zuzana Durkacova, both really great

QA Managers who always supported me with a huge amount of trust.

Big Kudos for Team Jupiter (formerly IO) for every lesson regarding Back-end, Front-end, API, or programming in general. To senior Java developer Ondrej Scecina (also Lead, Architect, and DevOps), thank you for being always ready to help. To all back-end guys: Radoslav Balucha, Gabriel Mohnansky, Jozef Jalc (JJ), and Jozef Chvostal (JC). To front-end king Alexander Petrik, and for our UI support from Adam Tabacko. And Zuzana Fornadlova, our Scrum Master, thank you for your great amount of tolerance and patience with us.

Big Kudos for all my remote colleagues in San Diego, but also for my current and previous colleagues and fellow testers both in Ness and Global Logic. Keep on with the development of Amazing projects regarding Energy, Sports, Security, Transportation, and especially Life-Saving projects, Machine Learning improvements, Augmented Reality and many more. You are all awesome.

A sincere thank you for Ondrej Palkoci, for all your Machine Learning tips and insights during our lunch breaks. You were a great friend during college, awesome roommate, and classmate. Good luck with your interests in Virtual and Augmented reality, creating a huge number of POCs, and hopefully you will soon have a successful business. Keep on with the amazing work, you have my support.

For Artificial Intelligence study materials belongs a big thanks to Stefan Tomasik, who studied cybernetics and mechanical engineering – but it still wasn't enough for the company, so he went on with an additional three years of academy extension. Good luck with your upcoming projects.

Thanks to every designer, researcher, coach or mentor who provided their arts, advice, code, insights, throughout my studies, coding, and writing.

Last, but not least, many thanks for all the support to everyone, who wished me good luck and hoped this book would become a great success.

I realize that each level of automation deserves a separate book. If a bigger interest would arise, I might write sequential books addressing each specific level, with deeper insights. Let me know your feedback, and I will keep you posted.

www.ingramcontent.com/pod-product-compliance
Lightning Source LLC
Chambersburg PA
CBHW041141050326
40689CB00001B/440